three tips

FOR CAMPUS SURVIVAL

Holding on to Your Faith
Through Your College Experience

CHUCK RYOR

What They're Saying About
THREE TIPS FOR CAMPUS SURVIVAL

"I think 'Three Tips for Campus Survival' is misnamed. Chuck hasn't given us a book about merely surviving life as a Christian on a college campus. Taken seriously, it will lead to thriving! Filled with personal antidotes, gospel wisdom and practical helps, Chuck shows us he's neither naïve nor a naysayer about the spiritual journey our sons and daughters face during their college years. A congregation would be wise to give a copy of 'Three Tips' to every one of its graduating seniors."
Scotty Smith, Founding Pastor
Christ Community Church – Franklin, TN

"With directness and insight, Chuck Ryor brings his extensive experience as a source of training and encouragement for Christian students. The three essential principles he outlines with provocative clarity can be applied well beyond the confines of a college experience. This is a great resource that will benefit all students preparing for college and many more people besides."
Rob Norris, Senior Pastor
4th Presbyterian Church – Bethesda, MD

"Chuck Ryor climbs right inside the head and heart of college students. His words are winsome, wise, witty and weighty. Every Christian kid leaving home needs this book. Every Christian school should make it required reading for college bound seniors."
Bob Evans, Senior Pastor
Wildwood Church – Tallahassee, FL

"With his sense of humor and direct communication style, Chuck Ryor is simply the most effective communicator to college students I have met. These practical, Biblical tips will help you as a student to grow in Christ and be a courageous Christ follower on campus. I highly recommend this book to you and the man who wrote it!"

Mark Millman, Missions & Church Planting Director
Central Baptist Association – Madison, WI

"Through my 21 years of campus ministry work with students from dozens of campuses from the community college to the Ivy League, the challenge remains the same. How can I help students to walk by faith and effectively communicate their faith in the face of the myriad obstacles and forces set to derail their commitment to Christ? Through the stories of those who have emerged from the college campus with their faith firm and full, 'Three Tips' will equip you with the practical foresight to anticipate and prepare for the inevitable tests to your convictions and character. I'd love to get this book in the hands of every high school senior and entering college freshman so that they can benefit from the hard experiences of others and choose a path that will propel their faith rather than compromise it."

Steve Baker, Philly Metro Director
Campus Crusade for Christ – Philadelphia, PA

"As a former Youth and College Pastor I can attest to the dearth of resources for our young people – this is a real gem. But the fact is that this is a book for everyone – because it comes from the heart of a man who loves Christ and who has never lost the wonder of his youth. Chuck speaks our native language – and I suspect we need that voice."

Mike Khandjian, Senior Pastor
Chapelgate Presbyterian Church & School – Baltimore, MD

three tips

FOR CAMPUS SURVIVAL

Holding on to Your Faith
Through Your College Experience

CHUCK RYOR

Foreword by Dr. Steve Brown
Author, Professor and Key Life Radio Bible Teacher

RED
MOUNTAIN
BOOKS
www.redmbooks.com

Requests for information should be addressed to:
RED MOUNTAIN BOOKS
2000 Mallory Lane, Suite 130-343
Franklin, Tennessee 37067
888-713-0343
www.redmbooks.com

ISBN #978-0-615-31449-5

Scriptures taken from the Holy Bible, New International
Version®, NIV®.
   Copyright © 1973, 1978, 1984 by Biblica, Inc.™
   Used by permission of Zondervan.
   All rights reserved worldwide.

Barna Research used by Permission of The Barna Group.

Quotations from *Connecting* by Larry Crabb and from *Morning &
Evening* by Charles Spurgeon used by Permission of Zondervan.

Printed in the United States of America.

For Nick and Holly

Stay connected with Chuck and the other members of the THREE TIPS Team through

THREETIPS.COM!

Register online for <u>FREE</u>.

Connect with others, get Three Tips gear and gather important campus survival resources.

- Chuck's Weekly College Blog
- Student Stories from around the country
- "Chick Tips" from female campus leaders
- LIVE Q & A online
- Random Tips and interviews from campus leaders throughout the U.S. and the world

SIGN UP TODAY AND STAY CONNECTED TO YOUR ONLINE SOURCE FOR CAMPUS SURVIVAL TIPS!

three tips

FOR CAMPUS SURVIVAL

CONTENTS

Acknowledgements

There are a few people I want to thank for their assistance in making this book possible. I'd like to thank my friends and partners in publishing, Brian Johnston and Lisa Starwalt of Red Mountain Books. I appreciate your willingness to go out on a limb of faith in this effort to help prepare God's children for college life. Thanks for partnering with me.

Secondly, thank you to Tara Gardner, my editor. You have been an amazing source of encouragement to me during this project. Your husband has been helpful, too.

Also, thanks to Panera Bread Co. of Pasadena. They have no idea I've been writing this book in their restaurant, but I owe them a shout out for the many hours of free internet and iced tea refills. I did pay for the first iced tea.

Finally, I've held it together these last two decades primarily because of God's grace given to me through two people: my wife, Carolyn, and my mentor, Rev. Mike Khandjian. I thank the Lord that He's given me these two, my "Pantaverate Buddies" and so many other good friends and family members to strengthen and encourage me along the path of following Jesus Christ. I love you all.

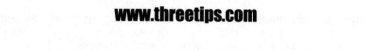

Foreword by Dr. Steve Brown
Author, Professor and Key Life Radio Bible Teacher

Someone has said God is good in that he timed the leaving of teenagers for college or university to coincide with the inability of their parents to answer their questions, clean their kids' rooms anymore, and abide their choice of clothes and entertainment any longer.

There is some truth to that.

If you're a parent whose kids are headed for the college or university campus you need to reconcile yourself to the fact that your paycheck is reduced, your "nest" is empty and you're going to worry . . . a lot.

And if you're the one leaving, you can hardly wait to get out from under the authority of your parents who you think know less than you do, don't understand you, and are far too concerned about you, your safety and your life than they need to be. However, because you're entering a place you've never been and encountering experiences you've never encountered, you are also going to worry . . . a lot.

A little advice from an old guy who has been there, done that and has a number of sweaty T-shirts.

Read this book!

In fact, it's about time that someone wrote a book like this—practical, clear, compassionate, wise and incredibly helpful.

I have a friend who tells parents that all they have done for their children is to give them a compass. No matter where they go or what they do, they won't be able to get rid of the compass and the compass will always point "home." This book is a survival guide in which the elements of that "compass" are described and taught in a way that will make an incredible difference.

And then just a word to the students who read what follows:

Nobody expects you're going to do it right all the time. Your parents didn't and you won't either. But when it gets messy and God seems to have gone on vacation, pick up this book, read it and underline it. When that happens you'll...

Rise up and call my friend, Chuck Ryor, blessed.

Steve Brown
Orlando, Florida
www.keylife.org

Author's Note

I've been ministering to college students for a long time. This "Survival Guide" wouldn't be worth much if the student stories weren't true. They are. However, in the interest of protecting the anonymity of individuals and saving them from embarrassment, I have changed some of their names.

Even as I relay their sometimes tragic demises, I want to be clear that I love and have empathy for these students. In college, I was an expert at one thing: moral weakness. If degrees had been handed out for a lack of moral fiber, I'd have graduated from college Summa Cum Laude and been a Rhodes Scholar. By no means do I consider myself to be morally superior to those whose failures I highlight along with my own. Instead, my responsibility to you is to humbly admit where I've messed up and tell the common tales of college students who've fallen into the same snares. This book is written to combine their stories with my own to help you avoid the dangers that exist on the college campus.

Chuck Ryor,
Pasadena, California
www.threetips.com

www.threetips.com

INTRODUCTION

Ally's Story

Ally was from south Florida. She was tanned, toned, and a big hit with the young Christian men during her first semester at our campus ministry in Tallahassee, Florida. She came to Florida State University from a private Christian school that sent over twenty students each year to one of Tallahassee's universities.

By all accounts of those who knew her at home, Ally was a committed believer in middle and high school. One guy in our ministry was from the same town as Ally and described her as a "Bible-toting Geek." That description was in stark contrast to where she ended up. She had a quality Christian education from kindergarten through 12th grade, her parents were devoted Christians who raised her to know the Lord, and she attended Bible studies and retreats with her youth group all the way up through her first semester in college. Despite all of this, Ally came to college and walked away from the faith of her youth.

Within a year of being on campus, she was best known as a finalist at a local bar's annual "bikini contest." Her scantily clad modeling pictures circulated through the social networking websites and began to be featured in print and television advertising. Ally was a fixture in the party scene around town, even working as one of the "sexy" bartenders at a local nightclub. In spite of multiple efforts to reach out to her, she continued her avoidance of all things spiritual. The last I heard of her, Ally was working as a waitress at Hooter's.

I had been a Christian for a while and a student pastor for a few years, but Ally's story was my first exposure to this depth of faith abandonment. My heart broke for how lost she was, and when I saw her around campus I would ask her how she was and invite her to continue coming to our fellowship while she sorted out her life. She rejected many attempts by students and staff to reel her back in. It made me sad to think about what her parents were going through.

I had seen students spend a semester partying and then cease doing so because they realized the error of their ways. I had seen many students in both high school and college go out with someone who was completely wrong for them and experience the consequences of bad decisions. But to my memory, this was the first completely Christian educated, high school youth group leader, "properly parented" student that I had seen to take such a spiritual 180. Sadly, it wouldn't be the last. Ally ended up isolated from other believers, continuously in situations that presented her with temptations that she was unable resist, and these environments couldn't help but to alter her understanding of what her relationship with God was all about.

Why A Survival Guide?

I have always loved the college campus. In addition to the love I have for my alma mater (West Virginia University in Morgantown, West Virginia), I have been a pastor and ministered to college students for nearly two decades. For all of its fun, there are genuine dangers involved in going to college. For all of its opportunities, few environments are as spiritually challenging for the Christians who live there as the college campus.

Why is that so? Two significant reasons: (1) It is often a new set of trials, temptations, and challenges for the 18-22 year-old man or woman, and first time experiences are daunting compared to the ones where you have had previous experience. (2) These new challenges come at the student from a variety of directions and in a myriad of ways: with whom you'll live, what you'll believe, and how you'll live your life.

After watching Christian students come and go from the state university campus for a long time, I've noticed that most—

regardless of the quality of their home life or church life—come to college completely unprepared for the barrage of spiritual challenges. Being a Christian in college, even at a Christian college, is an incredibly challenging endeavor. It is spiritually dangerous. It is complicated.

Over the years I've heard some parents and Christian pastors speculate that what causes students to fall away from faith is a shallow understanding of Scripture and theology. In some cases this may be true. However, I have seen little differentiation between the frequency of faith abandonment in the theologically informed and those whose faith was elementary in its understanding. As well, my experience has been that all students fall away from their faith for a few of the same basic reasons.

For those who are spiritually prepared for college, it can be one of the most exciting adventures of their lives, filled with memories and relationships that will last for a lifetime. Fundamental to that preparation is knowing and following a few basic rules or tips.

Tips for a Beginning Hiker

Outside of our home in Los Angeles' San Gabriel Valley is a magnificent view of the San Gabriel Mountains, and I wanted to experience them up close and firsthand. The problem was that I had never hiked a day in my life. These mountains were, in places, steep and known to possess all sorts of animals that I feared "unfriendly" to my survival.

Given the inherent dangers of hiking in the mountains, beginning hikers are given lots of advice. However, again and again three tips were offered to me so as to maximize my safety and enjoyment. This conventional wisdom can be applied not simply to hiking recreationally, but to anyone trying to climb even the highest peaks in the world.

TIP #1: Never go alone

If you are injured while hiking alone, there is no one to help you make it back, no one to call for help. You stand a much better chance scaring off a bear in groups, and with many eyes you can easily spot danger lurking in the bushes. I can speak for myself, but would you seriously consider hiking in unknown woods alone in the dark? I wouldn't. Come to think of it, there are very few places I'd go all alone, late at night, but especially unknown and potentially dangerous places.

TIP #2: Never Overestimate Your Ability

If you're a beginner, it is imperative that you recognize that you are a beginner. Frequently, pride will get the best of new hikers and they will try to climb higher than they are able and get altitude sickness. Some adventurous new hikers will see rock formations that they've watched people scale on TV and foolishly imagine that it is easy. Injury and death await the person who overestimates his or her own abilities.

TIP #3: Never leave the path

The snakes and other animals hide in the brush. There would be no danger if the animals put up signs along the path to alert you to their presence. Also, if you are a beginning hiker, you probably don't know your way around the area. Leaving the path could cause you to get lost, and every year we read stories of people who left the path to boldly go where they had never gone before, only to find that they couldn't get back. It is easy to lose your bearings when you are off the path, and those can be scary and deadly times for some hikers.

Your Collegiate Adventure

I liken these hiking principles to the three tips given in this book. Principles that will serve you well as you take on the challenges of the campus. Think of attending college like the thrilling opportunity to scale Mount Everest, the highest elevation on the planet. Recognizing the inherent dangers in life's adventures does not ruin them. Instead, it enhances the experience and enables you to live through it to tell the story to others.

Over the years, I've seen students arrive on campus hoping to climb the "Mount Everest of college experiences." Instead of recognizing how freezing cold the journey up the mountain is, they dressed for the adventure in shorts, t-shirts, and sandals. Most of the new Christian college students I've known are totally unprepared for the challenges and dangers that they'll face.

If you are going to survive the avalanche of temptations that are soon coming your way, you will have to know exactly what you can and cannot do, what you are able to resist and unable to say no to, and know ahead of time where you ought not be. It is sad how many Christian students completely overestimate how strong they are and how able they will be to resist the very real temptations of campus life. Not knowing your limitations could cost you dearly.

The path is there for your protection. In Christian terms, walking the "narrow path" is not necessarily just about obeying the rules. Lifestyle concerns and moral imperatives could be categorized this way. But for the Christian college student, knowing the path is more fundamentally about being clear about what you believe. If you are on solid ground about what you believe regarding God and His Word, you'll be far less swayed by the wide range of new and often threatening challenges to your faith. Before you can walk the path, you have to be clear in your own mind what exactly that path is.

Andrew's Story

One of the first high school students I ministered to was a young man named Andrew. When Andrew graduated from college, he fulfilled his ROTC commitment by serving as an Army pilot. Andrew was plenty intelligent, but he played football in high school and college and was so popular that he was never truly motivated to excel in academics.

Things were different in helicopter training school. He applied himself so diligently to his studies that he was the top pilot in his unit. As a result, he received a coveted invitation to fly fixed wing airplanes, a privilege offered only to the top helicopter pilots. At fixed wing school, the results were the same. He was the ace of his class and very quickly rose to leadership roles. At a young age, Andrew was an officer in charge of large groups of service men and women, some considerably older than he was.

So what was the difference in Andrew's approach to studying? Why did he excel at the highest level in Army pilot training compared to his high school and college educations? You might guess that he had more time as an adult than he had when he was in high school and college. But that's not it, as he had a family by the time he entered training and he would say that family requires more attention and focus than intercollegiate athletics.

So what was it? Three words: OPERATION IRAQI FREEDOM. Andrew was in training during war time. Nothing motivates someone to take their military training more seriously than the promise that very soon afterward an actual enemy will be shooting missiles in their direction. The stakes are even higher for pilots, who must add flying multi-million dollar planes into the mix of combat pressure.

While going to college isn't exactly like going to war, the principles of preparation for the unexpected and dangerous still apply. Unlike a soldier at war who would approach a sandy mine field with a map and walk carefully through the bombs, many Christian students play beach volleyball in the spiritual mine field and seem surprised when something disastrous happens. Perhaps it's because they didn't know these dangers lurked beneath the surface of their fun and games. My experience has been that many Christian students don't want to know; they enjoy the naiveté of approaching the party scene or Greek life as if it's a relaxing stroll through a botanical garden instead of a tip-toe through a series of life-threatening explosive devices. The results aren't pretty.

A 2006 Barna Group study shows that, despite being very active in church during their teen years, "twenty-somethings" are abandoning the faith of their youth in larger numbers than ever. "In total, six out of ten twenty-somethings were involved in a church during their teen years, but have failed to translate that into active spirituality during their early adulthood."[1] I believe that, for many people, the dismantling of their faith begins in college.

Many students find out too late that the faith they claimed to have wasn't really their own. They realize they can't define Christianity in any clear way, or even if they can define it, they discover that their faith isn't genuine.

The good news is that there is hope. When college-aged believers abandon their faith, there are often common patterns of

---

[1] "Most Twentysomethings Put Christianity on the Shelf Following Spiritually Active Teen Years." Barna Group; http://www.barna.org

behavior and explanations. Scripture says, "No temptation has seized you except what is common to man" (*1 Corinthians 10:13*) and that no experience from generation to generation is a new one — there is "nothing new under the sun." (*Ecclesiastes 1:9*).

Jesus explains to us how to make it through life's storms. At the conclusion of the Sermon on the Mount, he gives us a final tidbit about the need to apply what He says to our lives. *Matthew 7:24-27:*

"Therefore everyone who hears these words of mine and puts them into practice is like a wise man who built his house on the rock. The rain came down, the streams rose, and the winds blew and beat against that house; yet it did not fall, because it had its foundation on the rock. But everyone who hears these words of mine and does not put them into practice is like a foolish man who built his house on sand. The rain came down, the streams rose, and the winds blew and beat against that house, and it fell with a great crash."

According to Jesus, the key to spiritual survival is not only hearing God's Word but putting it into practice. Here's hoping that this collegiate spiritual survival guide, based on what the Scriptures teach, will assist you through this season of life. My prayer is that through reading this book, you'll realize exactly what a faith-challenging adventure you are taking on as you leave for campus.

I also pray that if your faith has been something you have not truly embraced for yourself, if it has been for show in order to make yourself appear moral to others, that this book will bring you into a fresh encounter with God's grace and love. Regardless of how many "tips" one has for spiritual survival, if you don't genuinely know, enjoy, and want to please God, you'll not have the gumption to follow any tips His Word has to offer.

I pray that, through a clearer understanding of what Jesus means to those who know Him and through the power of His Holy Spirit, you will read this book and discover the relationship of joy and freedom that His grace provides for genuine believers.

This book is written for the purpose of keeping you from being one of those who looks back and wonders, "How did I get away from what I used to believe?" But you'll first have to ask some hard questions of yourself, such as "Do I really understand what I've claimed to friends and family that I believe?"

Tip #1: NEVER GO ALONE

Be With Others as You Travel the Path

And let us consider how we may spur one another on toward love and good deeds. Let us not give up meeting together, as some are in the habit of doing, but let us encourage one another — and all the more as you see the Day approaching.
Hebrews 10:24-25

Though one may be overpowered, two can defend themselves. A cord of three strands is not quickly broken.
Ecclesiastes 4:12

"Friendship is unnecessary, like philosophy, like art... It has no survival value; rather is one of those things that give value to survival."
C. S. Lewis

"At Rex Kwan Do, we use the buddy system. No more flying solo. You need somebody watching your back at all times."
Rex from Napoleon Dynamite

My Real Friends

My freshman year in college, I met a senior by the name of Brian. He was tall, good looking, popular in the journalism school, and a professing Christian. He was also in a social fraternity. We took a class together, and I got to spend some time talking with him about journalism and Jesus. One day, when I asked him why he didn't come to our campus fellowship meetings, I was surprised when he responded that it was because he didn't like the people. Actually, what he sarcastically said was, "They're the kind of people I'd go shopping with." In other words, he was too cool to hang out with the nerds in our group. Obviously, my present company was excluded from his judgment!

As I watched his life from a distance, I could see that being popular was a priority of Brian's. Having cool friends was more important than having friends who would encourage him spiritually. I didn't confront him on this because he was older than me by three years. However, at the time I was offended by his comment because my campus fellowship was the only thing standing between me and loneliness as a college Christian.

I also must humbly admit that Brian's story was my own before I got to college. I partied with my non-Christian friends and went to church so I could confess that I had been partying. I enjoyed the idea of being a Christian and had moments of spiritual growth, but I was more concerned about being liked by the "in crowd" and being around that which was considered cool. Needless to say, my high school years were filled with many regrets and spiritual failures, mostly because I didn't have people around me who would encourage me to resist temptation and pursue my relationship with the Lord. Then I met Kay.

Kay was a girl in my class who I had not been too inclined to date because she wasn't in the "popular" crowd. She wasn't a cheerleader like my two previous girlfriends, and we didn't have the same circle of friends. But our lockers were near each other and we had some classes together, so we talked occasionally.

The summer before my senior year of high school, I ran into her and something was different. It wasn't just that she looked a lot hotter than I remembered, but there was also a change in her countenance. Kay was more energetic and vibrant. So I asked her out. I didn't know at the time that Kay was a Christian, and a newly enthusiastic one at that.

After a date or two, she and her church friends determined that she would bring me to her youth group, and if I didn't like it, she was going to end the relationship. The night she brought me to her church for the first time would change my life. I knelt down at the altar that evening and committed my life to Jesus, to be His disciple, and to follow His leadership for my life. Up to that point I had been a superficial Christian at best, easily swayed by the temptations of the party crowd with whom I ran around.

Over the following months, I was so excited to meet others who were energetic about their faith that I didn't bother to ask if they played sports or wonder if they were "cool" at their school. In fact, the people I began to enjoy the most were not athletes and very intentionally not part of the "in crowd" at their respective schools. It was this experience in my senior year of high school that paved the way for me to embrace my college Christian fellowship.

As a high school Christian with one foot in and one foot out of the faith, I had partied and failed and said I was sorry for my indiscretions over and over again. I had attempted to live the Christian life without the benefit of other believers by my side. By the time I got to college, I knew that I couldn't make it without some help. I needed other Christ followers in so many ways that I didn't care what I was missing out on while I spent time with my Christian brothers and sisters.

In an unexpected way, God used the foolishness of my high school years to prepare me for a myriad of new temptations that were headed my way. When my feet hit the ground in Morgantown, West Virginia, I knew from past failures that I was a Christian man who was vulnerable to the campus's spiritual dangers. And in spite of what some say, Christians don't have to "sow our wild oats" at some time. I've known lots of believers who never had a time of rebellion in high school or college, and they were healthier for not doing so.

Pride Goes Before the Fall

Pride goes before destruction, a haughty spirit before a fall.
Proverbs 16:18

Pride makes us think we can take on the spiritual adventure alone. An ambitious yet naïve mountain climber with the opportunity to summit Mount Everest is likely to be tempted to ignore warnings of an oncoming storm. Even with the knowledge that hundreds of experienced mountaineers have died on the mountain, the temptation to take risks for the once-in-a-lifetime chance to get to the top of the world is understandable. And this is why Everest climbers need not just good judgment, but they need to trust the people around them. Without the base camp director watching the weather, many more would die each year trying to summit the world's largest mountain.

I can usually tell when a college student is in trouble. Like an animal that wanders away from the pack and is eventually eaten by predators, these students disappear from our fellowship. Sometimes they disappear to move to another student ministry or church, but this is also a signal that they don't like the accountability of their current friends or pastors. It's easier to go to some other Christian group where no one really knows what they're up to. Church or Christian group "hopping" is a common but unhealthy practice among Christian college students. Real trust, genuine accountability, and in-depth friendships only happen over time. If you keep shortcutting what God is doing in your life to go where the transient mob is worshipping this semester, you will miss out on some of the greatest aspects of being part of a church or ministry.

However, most of the time, college students disappeared from our ministry when they started drinking alcohol heavily and didn't want to stop, or when they were dating someone with whom they were engaged sexually and had no intention of ending the relationship. This makes a lot of sense to me, as whenever I'm struggling with a besetting sin (one where I cannot seem to submit to God and obey), the last thing I want to do is be around other Christians who want to talk about it.

During one season of my college life, I fell in love with a Christian woman from our campus ministry. Up until the time we started fooling around sexually, I was an active leader in our campus ministry. The Bible study I led was exciting to me and affecting others, and I was regularly sharing my faith with anyone who was even remotely interested in hearing about it. Then the sexual activity began to dominate my dating relationship, producing guilty feelings in me but no real intention of changing my behavior.

In order to live in that world of compromise, I had to begin to artfully dodge places where the subject might come up. All of a sudden, I was always too busy to go to Bible study. I often cancelled the Bible study I led, or instead encouraged a time of extended prayer so we wouldn't have to talk about what was really going on. I had to lie to my spiritual mentor, because I knew that if I was truthful with him, he would challenge me to end the relationship. So I started avoiding him, too.

The first sign that things aren't going well in the life of a college student is when they start going at it alone. Be sure of this: God never wants you to live the Christian life alone. We were not made to live life alone (see Adam and Eve in *Genesis 1-2*), let alone our spiritual lives. From Genesis to Revelation, the spiritual life is lived in and amongst other followers of God.

You might respond, "Okay, what if you're spiritually mature? Doesn't God often make you stand alone then?" The answer is an unequivocal "No!" Adam had Eve. Moses had Aaron. The apostles had each other. God's people have always had to humbly recognize their need for each other. In the book of Acts, there is an implied group on every page because Luke himself (the one who wrote the Acts historical account) was present to witness and participate in the Acts of the Apostles. Throughout Acts, we see Christians going to jail together, going on missions together, praying together...all of it TOGETHER! Genuine spiritual maturity is not the absence of need for others; it is the humility to recognize your inability to make it alone.

Psychologist and author Dr. Larry Crabb writes:

I have come to believe that the root of all our personal and emotional difficulties is a lack of togetherness, a failure to connect that keeps us from receiving life and prevents the life in us from spilling over onto others. I therefore believe that the surest route to overcoming problems and becoming the people we were meant to be is reconnecting with God and with our community.[2]

Attempting to try to spiritually go alone not only affects you, it affects others in your community. Logs cannot burn very hot in the cold without being tightly packed with other pieces of wood. In the same way, Christians have little chance of burning with white hot passion for Jesus Christ without the benefit of having each other close by.

---

[2] Crabb, Larry, Connecting (Nashville, TN: Word Press, 1997), pg. 32.

The Myth of the Superhero

Since my college years, there have been a number of scandals involving very public Christian teachers and authors, often thought of as "Super Christians." When I was younger, these public falls from grace were shocking to me and many of my friends. They don't surprise me anymore because I see in Scripture that God's leaders have always had tragic flaws, gross weaknesses, and besetting sins. Many of these struggles have kept them humble and dependent on God as they labored on His behalf. Additionally, when you get the back story about how these modern day Christian superstars were living their lives, it should raise your suspicions about their lack of humility.

In one such instance in 2006, a nationally known minister was caught in a male prostitute and drug scandal and, consequently, had to resign as the pastor of his mega-church and as the leader of a powerful national Christian organization. By this evangelist's own admission, he would retreat monthly to another city by himself. He would leave his wife and family in his home town and hole up in an expensive hotel ostensibly to write books. And there he would be all by himself, alone in a city where (he thought) no one knew who he was. Like many who went before him and will unfortunately go after him, this man erroneously thought he could go alone.

IN HER OWN WORDS
Cynthia, Muskingum College Graduate
New Concord, OH

I grew up in a conservative Christian home in rural New Jersey and was generally compliant by nature. I was quiet, studious, and active in my church youth group. When I set foot on the college campus, my spiritual health was not my highest priority. I assumed that I had this part of my life under control. I considered myself to be strong minded and not easily drawn into temptation. I wanted to experience all the freedom of being away from home, including the ability to do as I wished on Sunday mornings.

My slip away from weekly church attendance was gradual. The first weekend at school, I woke up on Sunday morning, got dressed for church, and went to look for someone to walk to church with. As I wandered the halls of my dorm, not a soul was awake. Feeling rather stupid, I climbed back into bed and slept until noon like the rest of my dorm mates. My roommate and I talked about going to church, but we seemed to always having an excuse for not attending. At first, I felt guilty because I had never missed a Sunday in my entire life. The guilt eventually subsided and my church attendance was rare, at best.

I decided to try the only campus ministry at our school. Everyone I talked to on my hall rolled their eyes at the idea of attending with me, but I eventually found someone who would give it a shot. After we determined never to go again, we justified our attitude by contending that we did not know anyone and felt awkward being there. We thought about trying it again later but never did. I arrogantly commented that they were not talking about real Christianity, that there was no talk of a real relationship with Christ. All they talked about was resisting the temptations of drinking and I proudly felt that the subject was beneath me, because, in my mind, drinking wasn't going to be a problem for me.

Exploring college social life was like being on a big playground. I attended fraternity parties on the weekends and joined a sorority. Midway through my first semester, a senior football player expressed interest in dating me. He was popular, good looking, and I was flattered by the attention.

While I was his new love interest, the relationship was just a flirty game to me because I knew I wanted to marry a committed Christian. However, the relationship meant much more to him. I went along for the ride until he became possessive, jealous, paranoid, and obsessed with marrying me. Though it was difficult to do so and he resisted, I ended the relationship as my freshman year concluded.

Throughout my sophomore and junior years I partied hard, drinking heavily with my friends. I didn't want any commitment to a boyfriend and certainly not to God. I just wanted to have fun with my girlfriends and have a good time. Graciously, God protected me during this time in spite of some very stupid decisions on my part. Even though I was wandering far from Him, He was clearly still pursuing me. It was not until my senior year at Muskingum that the college social scene began to seem silly to me and I started to feel very alone. I longed for the relationship I once had with my Father in Heaven.

Finally, one Sunday during my senior year, I returned to a worship service and sat by myself, crying, and recommitting myself to pursuing a relationship with the God who would not let me go. I never imagined that I would one day end up so far from the pursuit of God, but when someone starts thinking they can live as a Christian without the help of other Christians, as I did, it is just a matter of time before they make the same discovery: we're not able to live it alone.

I can also say that God was faithful to hold on to me even as I was letting go of Him. He lived in me and allowed me to experience the pain of emotional distance from Him so I would return to Him with my entire heart. He forgave me of my many sins and restored me to the joy of my salvation.

That's why I have always loved King David's *Psalm 51:10-13*, which says:

"Create in me a pure heart, O God, and renew a steadfast spirit within me. Do not cast me from your presence or take your Holy Spirit from me. Restore to me the joy of your salvation and grant me a willing spirit, to sustain me. Then I will teach transgressors your ways, and sinners will turn back to you."

The first and second century Hebrew Christians were undergoing a persecution of monumental proportions. Former Jews who had publicly professed faith in Jesus Christ as the promised Jewish Messiah were being tortured unless they would recant their declarations. Most scholars agree that the book of Hebrews was written primarily to prevent "apostasy," the abandonment of the Christian faith, which is ultimately what the book you are reading now is about. This letter is written to a group of Hebrew Christians under intense pressure, and it is filled with encouragements to stay together. This is exactly what college students need to hear, too.

Keep on loving each other as brothers. Do not forget to entertain strangers, for by so doing some people have entertained angels without knowing it. Remember those in prison as if you were their fellow prisoners, and those who are mistreated as if you yourselves were suffering.
Hebrews13:1-3

Pray for us. We are sure that we have a clear conscience and desire to live honorably in every way. I particularly urge you to pray so that I may be restored to you soon. May the God of peace, who through the blood of the eternal covenant brought back from the dead our Lord Jesus, that great Shepherd of the sheep, equip you with everything good for doing his will, and may he work in us what is pleasing to him, through Jesus Christ, to whom be glory for ever and ever. Amen.
Hebrews 13:18-21

Being with other Christians isn't optional for the believer. We need others who have the presence of God's Holy Spirit in them to encourage us and "spur us on toward love and good deeds." *Hebrews 10:24-25* says, *"Let us not give up meeting together, as some are in the habit of doing, but let us encourage one another."* Apparently in the early church as is the case today, some Christians got in the habit of not being with others.

I've seen this a lot on the campus, students who simply get out of the practice of worshipping with others on Sundays or going to their weekly campus ministry meeting. Once you get used to an alternative schedule, it's really easy to stay in that mode. But it is critical for you to be places where you can make friends who understand the struggle of the Christian life, the temptations you face, and encourage you to love God and live in a way that pleases Him.

Two Blood Brothers – David & Jonathan

Some would say that if you have few good friends in your lifetime, you are a fortunate person. But if you have one true "blood brother" (or sister), someone who you'd give your life for and expect them to do the same for you...well, you are the most fortunate of people because those friendships are rare.

If you think only the weak and unremarkable need the intimacy of relationships of this quality, think again. Having close friendships is a human need that cannot be denied without a significant sense of loss and loneliness, and we're fortunate to have an example of such a friendship in the story of the manliest of men in the Old Testament.

King David of Israel was a former youngest son (low on the totem pole in ancient Israel), shepherd boy (low on the economic spectrum) turned giant-slayer and warrior extraordinaire in the service of King Saul. While living in the house of the king, David developed a tight relationship with the son of the king, Jonathan. They were fellow officers and war buddies, and both were part of the royal entourage. They spent a lot of time together.

While David was a gifted songwriter and poet, he was best known as a warrior. He was such a great warrior that the people became more impressed with David than they were with King Saul. David's fame so offended Saul that he decided he was going to kill him. Imagine your best friend's dad has decided to kill you. That type of family squabble would tend to put a crimp in a relationship between friends, but Jonathan and David's friendship was deep enough to endure even something this dramatic. Read this account in *1 Samuel 20:24-42* of how

Jonathan determined to betray his father to save his best friend. It's a long story, but it's worth it!

So David hid in the field, and when the New Moon festival came, the king sat down to eat. He sat in his customary place by the wall, opposite Jonathan, and Abner sat next to Saul, but David's place was empty. Saul said nothing that day, for he thought, "Something must have happened to David to make him ceremonially unclean — surely he is unclean." But the next day, the second day of the month, David's place was empty again. Then Saul said to his son Jonathan, "Why hasn't the son of Jesse come to the meal, either yesterday or today?"

Jonathan answered, "David earnestly asked me for permission to go to Bethlehem. He said, 'Let me go, because our family is observing a sacrifice in the town and my brother has ordered me to be there. If I have found favor in your eyes, let me get away to see my brothers.' That is why he has not come to the king's table."

Saul's anger flared up at Jonathan and he said to him, "You son of a perverse and rebellious woman! Don't I know that you have sided with the son of Jesse to your own shame and to the shame of the mother who bore you? As long as the son of Jesse lives on this earth, neither you nor your kingdom will be established. Now send and bring him to me, for he must die!"

Why should he be put to death? What has he done?" Jonathan asked his father. But Saul hurled his spear at him to kill him. Then Jonathan knew that his father intended to kill David. Jonathan got up from the table in fierce anger; on that second day of the month he did not eat, because he was grieved at his father's shameful treatment of David.

In the morning Jonathan went out to the field for his meeting with David. He had a small boy with him, and he said to the boy, "Run and find the arrows I shoot." As the boy ran, he shot an arrow beyond him. When the boy came to the place where Jonathan's arrow had fallen, Jonathan called out after him, "Isn't the arrow beyond you?" Then he shouted, "Hurry! Go quickly! Don't stop!" The boy picked up the arrow and returned to his master. (The boy knew nothing of all this; only Jonathan and David knew.) Then Jonathan gave his weapons to the boy and said, "Go, carry them back to town."

After the boy had gone, David got up from the south side of the stone and bowed down before Jonathan three times, with his face to the ground. Then they kissed each other and wept together—but David wept the most. Jonathan said to David, "Go in peace, for we have sworn friendship with each other in the name of the LORD, saying, 'The LORD is witness between you and me, and between your descendants and my descendants forever.'" Then David left, and Jonathan went back to the town.

In *2 Samuel 1:26*, after Jonathan died, David made this statement about his best friend: "I grieve for you, Jonathan my brother; you were very dear to me. Your love for me was wonderful, more wonderful than that of women." Contrary to some twisted scholarship on the subject, there was nothing sexual about this declaration. What you see in the relationship between David and Jonathan is mutual dependence between brothers in the Lord. It's this kind of relationship that God desires for you and this kind of friendship that you will need if you're heading into the spiritual battlefield that is the college campus.

Alex's Story

Alex was a college student from south Florida who was a home school student all the way up to his time at Florida State. Not long after going to FSU, Alex began to ask questions about how good his "good" friends from his home church were. This is another common experience that Christian students have. Somewhere in their first year on campus, they may correctly or incorrectly assess that they have better friends outside of their Christian community.

When we have the chance to meet new friends, some of whom aren't Christian believers but are really nice all the same, it is an exhilarating experience. These new relationships can put into perspective how intimate and genuine our past relationships were. In response to this often new experience, some Christian students will blame the poor quality of their Christian friendships on other people instead of taking a hard look at why they haven't been able to foster these types of relationships within their Christian communities. Ideally, the security we have in Christ should produce Christian friendships that are authentic and full of honesty and transparency.

If we really believe that Jesus has made us acceptable to the Father through His sacrifice on the cross, this should free our church friendships from insecurity and hypocrisy. Sadly, this is often not the case. Alex eventually found out what many Christians do: when people aren't Christians, they aren't spiritually empowered to say they're sorry when they screw up. They aren't compelled by the presence of God to admit fault or pursue reconciliation. They are selfish by nature, as are we, but they are unrestrained by God's grace.

Before I went to seminary and then into the ministry, I worked as a disc-jockey for several years at radio stations in a few different cities. At one station where I worked as a sports reporter in the morning show, I was particularly close to two people who were not professing Christians but were some of my best friends. They were funny, genuine, enjoyable to be with, and they cared for me.

But pressure reveals cracks. When things got tough at work, when conflict happened, when disagreements surfaced, these two would fight nastily with each other. When I had disagreements with them individually, I would pursue conflict resolution and generally achieve reconciliation. When they had problems with each other, they talked behind each other's backs but never to each other. Eventually, their inability to humbly resolve their conflicts led to the end of their working relationship and friendship. It was unfortunate because, as radio teams go, they could have been great.

One of my girlfriends in college was in a sorority, and each year they had a community ritual at the conclusion of "Rush Week" in which she played a role. Rush is the Greek system's semi-annual event when students and the fraternities and sororities check each other out to see if there is a good fit. It is a high pressure time for many young men and women where they are critically evaluated based on their looks, personality, looks, academic potential, looks, leadership qualities, and…did I mention they are evaluated on their physical appearance?

My girlfriend's sorority would offer "bids" to young women they considered worthy to be part of their Greek family, and at the first gathering with the new pledges, she would sing this beautiful song called "Family." The tears flowed and the hugs filled the room. The young women felt accepted; they had made the grade and were officially part of a group. Whatever else would happen that first semester, these girls would not lack for friends or social life. It was a thrilling moment for freshmen women, and for many Christian girls, it was the first time they had ever experienced this kind of emotional joy and intimacy with people not in their families. However, at my girlfriend's sorority it wasn't genuine.

Within a semester of holding hands and crying together at the initiation ceremony, within months of hugging the necks of those who were gracious enough to include the new girls in their club, these same women of the sorority "family" started acting like, well, human beings. They were backbiting, jealous, catty, and cruel. My girlfriend joined her sorority as a freshman, and during her junior year she became a Christian through the influence of another Christian woman in her house. When she quit partying, ceased keeping track of her sexual conquests on her sorority's "shack board," and started dating "Jesus Freak" guys like me, the "family" began to distance themselves from her.

It didn't take long for her and the other Christian girls in her sorority to realize that on the surface these relationships seemed genuine, but when push came to shove, all people are selfish. That's true for us, too. Without the restraining grace of God's Holy Spirit, without the conviction that He brings to us when we displease God the Father by hurting others, without the continual reminder of the sacrifice Jesus made on our behalf, we wouldn't desire to put others first either.

Do nothing out of selfish ambition or vain conceit, but in humility consider others better than yourselves. Each of you should look not only to your own interests, but also to the interests of others. Your attitude should be the same as that of Christ Jesus.
Ephesians 2:3-5

RANDOM TIP A
Time Management – You've got more time than you know

There is little argument that, in theory, your chief purpose for attending college is to get an education. However, most realize that there are so many extra-curricular activities clamoring for your attention and enjoyment that college is hardly a one-dimensional experience.

The problems start when you finish a semester and looking at your report card gives evidence that studying and going to class clearly weren't your top priorities. Whether it's your parents or guardian, Greek house, athletic department, or the ones who granted you the academic scholarship, you now have to answer for your bad grades.

My experience as a student, professor, and college pastor is that the major problem a student encounters in this regard is poor time management. It is important to remember two things so you can get the most out of your college experience and still keep parents happy with your grades. And if you apply these two random tips, you will enjoy yourself a great deal more than if you don't.

Random Tip A[1]: Remember that there are 168 hours in a week. If you take 15 hours of coursework each week, study 30 hours per week (2 hours for each hour in class), eat 21 hours per week (3 hours a day), and sleep 56 hours per week (8 hours a day), you still have 46 hours in your week left to do whatever else you need to do. If you are running out of time, you'll need to realize it's because you are wasting it somewhere.

Random Tip A[2]: Perhaps most importantly, you'll enjoy your free time more if you get your studying done first. Otherwise, your time with friends will always have a cloud of depressing thoughts hanging over it. Your mind will haunt you with thoughts like, "I've still got this test to study for" or "I still have to write that paper for class tomorrow." If you'll take the time to knock out your studying before you hang out with friends, you'll enjoy your free time without the burden of unfinished work. This formula might help, **THF[2]**: it means "Tackle Homework First" and "Then Have Fun."

Remember these words from King Solomon in *Proverbs 12:24:*
"Diligent hands will rule, but laziness ends in slave labor."

There is a tendency for some Christians to be judgmental of others and lack a depth of understanding about God's grace, which in turn can make being near them a disappointing relationship. But if you know what you believe (see Tip #3), and make certain that those you consider your Christian friends share the same convictions about humility and honesty, then you will discover that life without this kind of authentic fellowship isn't what God wants for us. Over the years I've experienced both wonderfully real and terribly phony Christian relationships. Once I encountered the real, I couldn't settle for anything else in my friendships.

Who Says You Can't Go Home?

One reason these social groups are so attractive to us is our innate need for familial connections. Most of us take for granted the presence of parents or siblings, never truly appreciating just how valuable they are and how much we've consciously or subconsciously depended on them. In the movie bearing his name, Wyatt Earp listened to his father teach him that "nothing counts as much as blood, the rest are just strangers." We all long for loyalty and for relationships that are unconditional in their love. Family is one place where we generally can find these things.

When students go off to college, many are without this bedrock of their lives for the first time. Homesickness causes many students to quit school and go home, and it isn't just the wimpy ones either. Even tough guys like football players are not immune, as we saw many times in Tallahassee when an athlete would return home after just a few weeks on campus. It is not uncommon for a new recruit to leave a team due to homesickness. And the more connected people are to their families, the more likely they are to be homesick. While we try to project independence and strength, inside we're desperate for close ties and faithful relationships.

This need for close relationships is intensified in students (statistically over 50% of them) who come from homes where there has been divorce. Without consciously realizing it, many young men and women who have lived amidst divorce, abandonment, or a home life that has been less than nurturing, crave relational loyalty and fidelity.

So it is understandable that the Greek system or the dorm crowd or the people with whom you work begin to scratch your soul's need for intimate connection. The catch is that if they don't know Jesus, if they've not experienced the grace He's extended in the gospel and they aren't secure in the knowledge that they are unconditionally loved by God, there is little or no chance they can extend unconditional love to you. It is axiomatic that one cannot accurately paint a picture of what one hasn't seen.

That is absolutely the case with regards to unconditional love. It is completely foreign to the human mind and heart and something that is rarely seen or experienced on this earth. We are naturally sinful and selfish and require the transforming grace, presence, and conviction of God's Holy Spirit. Without Him, we can do nothing and apart from His grace in our lives we would never be compelled to love others the way Jesus has commanded us to. Eventually, Christian students get to see the true quality of their friendships.

It took Alex a couple of years to figure this out, but he eventually realized that the grass isn't greener on the other side. Even if we have good friends who aren't Christians, it doesn't negate the need we have for spiritual encouragement. The Scriptures are clear that we need other believers, and to neglect the fellowship of believers is to disobey God and neglect the needs of our souls and the souls of other Christian brothers and sisters.

Hebrews 13:1 says, *"Keep on loving each other as brothers."* Paul was longing for not only the prayers of his brothers and sisters but their encouraging presence when he wrote in verses

18-19, *"Pray for us. We are sure that we have a clear conscience and desire to live honorably in every way. I particularly urge you to pray so that I may be restored to you soon."*

From a spiritual standpoint, I never would have made it safely through my college years without the genuine friendships that I had at my church and in our campus ministry. Over my years of ministry, I have watched some Christian students not simply "survive" but also thrive on the college campus, and every one of them had genuine Christian friendships that provided the strength they needed to make it.

Do you want to survive spiritually while away at school? Then make it your highest priority when you get to campus to find a Christian fellowship or a church with an active college group. Find a theologically reliable church that understands God's grace and the need you and I have for forgiveness from each other on a daily basis. Make a commitment to yourself that you will not join a fraternity or sorority until you have found a campus ministry—even if that means waiting a semester or a year to rush. And if you decide to go Greek, make sure the house you join has a Bible study that you can be welcomed into. It would also be helpful if you had a Christian friend who was willing to go through the process with you. Actively seek others to join you in your journey, for your good and for theirs.

Campus Ministries

Here are a few campus ministries that are usually available on most college campuses. You can visit their websites before leaving for school and contact their campus staff ahead of time. In the absence of one of these groups, check online in your school's city and visit local church websites. Comb through those church websites for their doctrinal statements and to find out whether they have programs for college students and people that you can contact.

Baptist Campus Ministry *www.bcmlife.net*

Campus Crusade for Christ *www.campuscrusadeforchrist.com*

Campus Outreach *www.campusoutreach.org*

InterVarsity Christian Fellowship *www.intervarsity.org*

Reformed University Fellowship *www.ruf.org*

The Navigators *www.navigators.org*

Stay connected with Chuck and the other members of the THREE TIPS Team through

THREETIPS.COM!

Register online for <u>FREE</u>.

Connect with others, get Three Tips gear and gather important campus survival resources.

- Chuck's Weekly College Blog
- Student Stories from around the country
- "Chick Tips" from female campus leaders
- LIVE Q & A online
- Random Tips and interviews from campus leaders throughout the U.S. and the world

SIGN UP TODAY AND STAY CONNECTED TO YOUR ONLINE SOURCE FOR CAMPUS SURVIVAL TIPS!

three tips
FOR CAMPUS SURVIVAL

IN HIS OWN WORDS
Peter, Florida State University Graduate
Tallahassee, Florida

I grew up in a Christian home. Maybe I didn't spend every Sunday in church, but my dad was a youth pastor for some years and taught us about the fruits of the Spirit and the fundamentals of having a relationship with Christ. We lived in a very isolated rural area for years, but when I was 14, we moved into a neighboring city—much larger than the intimate community I was used to. We found a church and started attending regularly.

I got involved with the youth group and I spent a lot of time attending programs and camps that they would have. I was a regular all through high school, and, as I transitioned into college, I volunteered with the high school and middle school groups, leading Bible studies and leading on ski trips and retreats. I did it all.

During my sophomore year in college, I started dating a girl that I met while playing guitar at a church event. She was great; infectious laugh, same taste in music and movies, and we were having a great time together. So great, in fact, that it was hardly noticeable that our relationship was spilling across sexual lines that I knew were dangerous, and eventually all the way across the line. We were really into each other, and it just felt so natural. Then reality hit.

A day before I was supposed to spend two weeks running security for a youth camp, I found myself driving to Wal-Mart at 3 a.m. to get a home pregnancy test. My girlfriend was freaking out and I was not doing much better. Our lives were flashing before our eyes—what had we done? The tests all came back negative, all except for one. She scheduled a consultation with a doctor the day I was shipping out for camp.

As much as I didn't want to go to camp, it turned out that some time in the woods watching for pranksters proved to be a good time for God to give me a potent heart-to-heart. Surrounded by people I had known for years, staying up 18 hours a day, and living on camp food really softened my heart and calmed me.

I knew what had to be done. More importantly, I knew what God's will was. When I returned from camp, things weren't as clean-cut as I'd hoped. While the doctor had confirmed that she was not pregnant, the weight of that event had leveled some unforeseen effects. When I told her that we should examine our direction and seek some counseling, she showed me a side that I'd not seen before.

She was weeping, incoherent, and making no sense. Our conversation was far from just heated. She alluded to wanting to kill herself and even attempted to do so that very evening. I was terrified. It was a very long night.

We parted ways much worse off emotionally and spiritually than either of us had ever been. I went down a road of heavy drinking, punctuated by drug use and a general disregard for my own health. My world was upended; my perceived layout of God's plan for my life was out the window; why not?

I lost several years to that mindset. But God was faithful—He let me close enough to the fire that my eyebrows took a while to grow back in, but He didn't let me go. I was even confused as to why he didn't just cut me off. I was an ungrateful, angry, dissonant spoiled kid. I worked really hard at trying to convince Him and myself that I wasn't worth keeping around, that if He could just let me go home (up there), things would be better. But there again, that was what *my* plan was.

It has been years since those days where I could have sworn that I had messed up bad enough to shatter God's plan for my life. As it turns out, that was pretty presumptuous of me, to say the least. Today, more than ever, I'm exceedingly grateful that He was in control the whole time, even though it didn't always feel like it. I have a loving wife, two wonderful kids, and a career that is truly a blessing. I've discovered that *Romans 8:38-39* is absolutely true:

For I am convinced that neither death nor life, neither angels nor demons, neither the present nor the future, nor any powers, neither height nor depth, nor anything else in all creation, will be able to separate us from the love of God that is in Christ Jesus our Lord.

www.threetips.com

Tip #2: NEVER OVERESTIMATE YOUR ABILITY
Be Humble as You Walk the Path

*So, if you think you are standing firm, be careful that you don't fall!
No temptation has seized you except what is common to man. And God
is faithful; he will not let you be tempted beyond what you can bear.
But when you are tempted, he will also provide a way out so that you
can stand up under it.*
1 Corinthians 10:12-13

*Remain in me, and I will remain in you. No branch can bear fruit by
itself; it must remain in the vine. Neither can you bear fruit unless you
remain in me.*
John 15:4

"A man's got to know his limitations."
Clint Eastwood as "Dirty Harry" in Magnum Force

Dating at a Psychologically Healthy Pace

During my sophomore year at WVU I took a self-paced psychology class. A "self-paced" class is one where you have a proctor for tests but no professor or lectures. Students are supposed to come to class prepared each week to take unit tests based on the weekly chapter readings. If you decided to take two tests a week, you can theoretically finish a fourteen-week class in seven weeks.

Like many other lazy students, I flipped that express plan on its ear and blew off tests for the first few weeks of class, ending up having to take a ton of tests in the last few weeks of the semester.

However, I did show up for class each week and it wasn't to take a test. Beginning the first week of class, a really cute girl smiled at me. Of course, I smiled back. My weekly routine in self-paced psych was to get to class early and smile at the cute girl who walked in after me. After a couple of weeks, she began to sit near me and we'd actually say "hi" to each other. Weeks of casual flirtation went by as she rapidly made her way through the coursework and I made it look like I was doing so. This girl was way out of my league, and she was paying attention to me. It was very exciting for an insecure guy.

So, What's the Problem?

As a college student who was also a Christian man, I had made a commitment not to date women who weren't Christians. To some, this seemed an unrealistic and slightly judgmental approach to dating. I made the commitment for two basic reasons. First, I wanted to get married and knew that if I fell in love with someone who wasn't a Christian, I risked disobeying the Scriptures and marrying someone with whom I was "unequally yoked." *2 Corinthians 6:14-15* says:

"Do not be yoked together with unbelievers. For what do righteousness and wickedness have in common? Or what fellowship can light have with darkness? What harmony is there between Christ and Belial? What does a believer have in common with an unbeliever?"

Over the years, I have seen the heartbreak of those who have legally bound themselves to those who work from a different set of beliefs and lack the same relationship with Jesus. Being "unequally yoked" refers to the harnessing together of two farm animals that work together to complete the tasks before them. When a bull is yoked with a horse, the stronger of the two overpowers the weaker and controls their direction, making it was difficult for the farmer to keep the plow moving the intended direction.

The Biblical admonition to be equally yoked is a command to bind ourselves only to those of the same kind so we can work together in obedience to our master, Jesus. Also, it is a picture of our weakness—not the weakness of the one to whom we're yoked. My commitment to date only believers was linked to my complete lack of faith in my moral strength. In the Biblical image, the unbeliever will take us places we don't want to go and we won't have the strength to resist.

This was the second reason I had for dating only Christian women: I was weak regarding all things sexual and needed all the help I could get—especially from a godly woman who I was certain wouldn't go for any fooling around. Sexual promiscuity is rampant in our culture, as it was 2,000 years ago. Hence, when we read in Scripture that "all temptation is common" and that "God is faithful to provide a way out" when tempted, that is as true for us today as it was for Christians in the sex-drenched Roman culture of the first century.

As if the world's barrage of sexual temptation wasn't challenging enough, we were wonderfully created by God to be sexual beings and to enjoy sex, and we need to have sex in order to procreate. The desire to have sex with someone you love or to whom you are attracted is as natural as breathing. While this is true, in Scripture God has clearly reserved sexual intimacy for the secure environment of a monogamous, committed, heterosexual marriage. Inside that marriage boundary, God doesn't say be passive about sex, but to pursue it with great passion. That's why *1 Corinthians 7:4-5* says:

The wife's body does not belong to her alone but also to her husband. In the same way, the husband's body does not belong to him alone but also to his wife. Do not deprive each other except by mutual consent and for a time, so that you may devote yourselves to prayer.

Just Powerful Enough to Kill You

I liken sexuality to the power of the atom. When nuclear technology is used properly, it can power cities and machinery, providing light and life to millions. That's how it is with sex. In the context of a relationship where you are secure, sexual intimacy is the closest thing to a heavenly experience we have on this earth. And it isn't just about the physical experience of an orgasm, it is about the joy of being physically, emotionally, and spiritually naked in the presence of another person and being completely secure.

When I was single I couldn't imagine that having sex with the same person for the rest of my life would get anything but boring over the years of marriage. I've discovered that the opposite is true, at least for my wife and me. What has made the difference for me? The main differences between my sexual experiences as a young person and the ones I've had since being married are the knowledge that I'm pleasing God with my life (no post-sex guilt), that I'm secure that my wife loves me and won't leave me (no relationship jealousy), and that my sexual enjoyment is linked to my wife's pleasure as much as my own. This last one was a drastic change from the illicit sexuality of my youth, where sex was about what I could take instead of what I could give.

While nuclear energy can power a city, it can also have a tragic, devastating impact when mishandled. No nuclear physicist, plant scientist, nuclear lab tech, or military serviceman has ever seen anything good happen from casually handling nuclear materials. And who would think of doing so? Only the ignorant would be unaware of the potential dangers inherent in this powerful resource.

Sex is no different, and you don't have to go very far to see the devastating effects on a culture and a people who have treated sex as careless recreation. It was true in my own life, with the fall out from my sexual promiscuity being broken hearts and jealousy-filled relationships of mistrust. For some of my sexually active friends, there were unexpected pregnancies and unwanted sexually transmitted diseases.

Perhaps the most dangerous threat to the sexual safety of many, however, is not a real life sexual experience but the draw of sexual fantasy that is stimulated by pornography. If your pre-college home environment has prevented this temptation from being a reality, get ready for a powerful new enemy.

RANDOM TIP B
Guard Your Soul from Internet Dangers

One of the big surprises many Christian men get when they arrive at college is a brand new set of temptations. Perhaps you didn't know it ahead of time, but most schools take that mandatory activity fee and provide high-speed internet in your dorm room. While this particular tip is primarily for college-aged men, it is a relevant discussion for women, too. At the very least women will understand all guys a little better. Not to say that there aren't women who are tempted to look at pornography as men are, but not the entire gender! One specific reason looking at sexual images is a temptation for most all Christian men is that God has hardwired the male of our species to have their strong sexual desires, and those desires are triggered through their eyes.

According to the Scriptures the Lord wants married men to pursue their spouses for procreation and for pleasure. It is not wrong for us to want sex. I wonder if there would be a human race if not for the sexual hunger of men. We should thank God that most if not all men are naturally obsessed with sex. However, as was mentioned previously, sex is a powerful force that can be harmful to the soul if misused. There is no end to the damage that internet pornography can and will do to your perspective on what sex is supposed to be all about.

Internet porn is a gigantic temptation because college students spend a significant amount of time online for school and for social networking, and much of that time is spent alone. To compound the difficulty, the issue of breaking the ice to discuss pornography addiction is hugely difficult for most Christian men. For many, it's just an embarrassing topic to bring up, especially in mixed company, so we tend to talk about our "struggles with lust" in general terms, if at all.

Dealing with pornography addiction with a group of friends requires a willingness to bare our souls, deliberate engagement of the topic in discussion, and the grace to encourage each other in our struggles. That engagement is grounded in a deep understanding of our own sinfulness and the grace that God offers through Christ. But it begins with somebody bringing up a difficult topic.

Wise students have a means of accountability to keep them from becoming pornography addicts. Having friends who will ask the tough questions will be helpful, but having a software program that promotes accountability will be even more so. One thing is certain; you'll need God and an honest group of friends to help fight this battle.

And God is Faithful

By the time I was 20 years old, I had sewn enough "wild oats" to at least realize in my head that reckless sex had bad consequences. But sexual desire and emotional affirmation are powerful forces, so when the attractive woman in my self-paced psych class started flirting with me, I figured "What's the harm?" Then, it happened. One day, midway through the semester, she finished her self-paced exam and, instead of walking out the door, she made her way toward me with a great smile on her face.

"Well, I'm all done. I've taken my last exam." She happily stated.

"I've got a long way to go, still," I replied. "So, are you going to come back and see us?" I wanted to continue our flirtation.

"No, I'm not coming back here. But I would like to see you sometime," she said as I nervously wondered what that meant. "Here's my name and number. Give me a call."

I think I knew what she meant. I was so shocked that I stammered something out and stared up and down at her as she walked away (another failure of judgment).

As fate would have it, I was all alone the very next Friday night. Sitting at my dorm room desk, I looked down at a scrap of paper with the name and the phone number of a great looking woman on it. For what seemed like a considerable length of time, I contemplated the pros and cons of calling my beautiful classmate.

"Maybe she just wants to be friends?" I justified to myself as I thought of picking up the phone. "She might be a Christian and we'd have a lot to talk about...you never know?"

As the minutes of temptation added up to an hour, I knew I was at a critical crossroad. I knew what my limitations were, and was sure that all it would take was isolation at a vulnerable location and willingness on the part of an attractive woman for me to head down a path of sexual disobedience to the Lord. As I contemplated whether I wanted to please myself or my Savior, I remembered the promise that at the moment of temptation, the Lord would provide a way out. Suddenly, I realized that the only way out was to get rid of the number, so I sprinted down the dorm hallway and into the restroom, wadded the dreaded piece of paper into a ball, and flushed it down the toilet.

At that moment I experienced a solemn joy, one that would last far longer than any single sexual encounter. It was the thrill of knowing that I had obeyed the Scriptures and brought pleasure to my heavenly Father. His Holy Spirit filled me with His presence and joy, and I spent the rest of that evening eating pizza in my dorm, reading the Scriptures, and enjoying God.

Lessons from the Corinthian Christians

Scripture promises that we can resist temptation and that God will provide a way out for us. *1 Corinthians 10:13* says, *"And God is faithful; he will not let you be tempted beyond what you can bear. But when you are tempted, he will also provide a way out so that you can stand up under it."* I truly believe that the biggest key to overcoming temptation is caution about the situations in which we place ourselves. If you and I are serious about obeying the Lord, we've got to be careful where we go and who we go there with. In the event that you or I foolishly walk into situations filled with temptations, God is still faithful to be with us and to guide us in paths of righteousness.

This was the struggle of the Christians in the New Testament city of Corinth where the Apostle Paul had established one of his first mission churches. This group of zealous Christians had experienced the grace of God, were particularly experienced in the supernatural manifestations of God's Holy Spirit, and zealously proclaimed the gospel to friends and foes alike. On the other hand, they also struggled with their vices. Sexual immorality was a regular part of their city, and illicit sexuality had found its way into the church community's practices.

On top of that, the Corinthians loved to party and get drunk, even at church. I'm sure that in the 21st century we all humbly recognize that our sin is pretty shameful and that there are contemporary situations that are embarrassing to the church. But when was the last time you heard about people getting hammered as part their church's communion service? Such was the condition of the Corinthian church community when Paul wrote to them to rebuke their callous unconcern for personal holiness and to provide them with some practical answers for dealing with temptation.

At our campus ministry in Tallahassee, we were often slandered for our perceived lack of concern for personal holiness. There were a couple of reasons that our ministry had that reputation. First, we were large and it is easy for folks to take shots at ministries that are big, because chances are that there is always a knucklehead or two in any group of over 300. We had some students who claimed to be Christians but always pushed the envelope of "personal freedom." There are always students who take advantage of a climate that is not legalistic, one that attempts to reach out to the non-churched by making the environment accessible and culturally understandable. On a number of occasions, we had to address those students who were pushing these freedoms to foolish limits.

On the other hand, I taught with clarity that people are not justified before God by their good works. Instead, our good works are the natural byproduct of a genuine conversion to Christianity, a relationship with God that is only possible because of our faith in the finished work of Jesus Christ. If a person did not truly want to please the Lord, I would have questioned whether or not that student was genuinely a believer.

Our ministry also recognized that people grow at different paces, and we were reluctant to quickly judge people before the Holy Spirit had the opportunity to convict them of their disobedience and draw them back to Himself by His grace. I would contend that making it safely through college would involve being in a campus ministry that strikes that all-important balance between grace and truth. We'll address this more later.

For now, it is critical that we remember that we are infinitely weaker than we want to believe. We're far too confident in our own ability to withstand temptation, and often we foolishly enter into situations that are far beyond our ability.

Two Friends Choose Poorly

There is this scene that I've always loved in *Indiana Jones and the Last Crusade.* At the movie's conclusion, both Indiana Jones and his adversary have to choose the chalice they believe to be the Holy Grail and drink water from it to see whether they've chosen correctly. Indy's enemy picks the fancy chalice that he presumes is fit for the King of Kings. When he drinks from the elaborate cup, his face melts and his head explodes. The ancient guardian of the Holy Grail gives a rather dry response: "He chose poorly."

That colossal understatement "he chose poorly" always makes me laugh. Then Indy picks up the rugged chalice, which he deems the cup of a humble carpenter, and his is declared a wise choice. His face doesn't melt and he lives for more Indiana Jones adventures.

Regarding our choices to place ourselves in harm's way, I've seen my share of students who have chosen poorly. I specifically think of two students, Josh and Ashley, who were part of my high school youth ministry and both went to college at FSU. I had such high hopes that their time in our college ministry would take them to new and exciting levels as Christian believers.

Unfortunately, they both made choices to jump into the Greek system without any healthy reflection about how it was going to affect their spiritual lives. Neither of them were particularly strong believers in high school. They said the right things and seemed excited to be part of the group, but they regularly (as I did in high school) fell prey to the party scene. As well, each of them also had dating relationships in high school that got out of bounds sexually.

I knew Ashley since she was in middle school, and I always had a soft spot in my heart for her. She was intelligent, attractive, funny, and courageous. She was raised in a Christian home, but she was negatively affected by her parents' divorce and more so by her father's lack of genuine emotional connection with her. I had great sympathy for why she struggled as she did.

Josh was special to me for a different set of reasons, mostly because we had so much in common. He was an athlete who became a Christian in high school, and he had a really sensitive side. He was tender and affectionate, loved his little sister whom he led to the Lord, and had a great relationship with his parents. His weakness was that he loved the party scene and the attention of really cute girls. Most guys can relate to his struggles.

That said, I advised students like Josh and Ashley to be sure that they knew what they were getting into. In their cases, they either didn't really care that there were risks to their spiritual lives, or they severely miscalculated their ability to resist temptation. Both drifted far away from the faith of their youth, and they did so mostly because of their inability to resist the temptations they faced. These temptations were central to their social lives at their respective fraternity and sorority houses.

Ashley dove headlong into the party scene. She dated a cute and popular guy who wasn't a believer, and when she broke up with him, he started stalking her. Josh was living a mirror existence across campus, as he started dating different young women who were beautiful and sexually aggressive. These two chose poorly, virtually setting themselves up for failure because they overestimated their own strength.

King David wrote in *Psalm 23:1-3*:

The LORD is my shepherd; I shall not be in want. He makes me lie down in green pastures, he leads me beside quiet waters, he restores my soul. He guides me in paths of righteousness for his name's sake.

David knew quite a bit about temptation. In spite of the fact that the Scriptures referred to him as a man after God's own heart, David regularly found himself battling temptations that are common for today's college students. On one occasion, he committed adultery with another man's wife and unexpectedly got her pregnant. Then, in an attempt to cover his tracks, David tried to get her husband to come home from battle and sleep with her so he'd think that he got her pregnant. When that failed, he orchestrated the death of his lover's husband. His confession and repentance from these sins is recorded in *Psalm 51*, where he wrote, *"Against you, you only, have I sinned and done what is evil in your sight."*

Even the most spiritual people, the ones we envy for their spiritual maturity, even they will succumb to temptation if they are not careful. As I mentioned earlier, David was the chosen King of Israel and the quintessential man: a warrior, a musician, a politician, and a spiritual leader. Yet he committed adultery and murder, and he was forgiven by God. I remind us of this so we can celebrate that our disobedience is never so excessive that God will not forgive us.

There may be consequences to our actions, but sometimes God even mercifully spares us from the results of our disastrous choices. In King David's case, he experienced the conviction of the Holy Spirit, but the ramifications for his family were devastating. His selfishness led to years of family infighting and disloyalty from other sons. However, it is important to point out that David's temptation, disobedience, and the resulting consequences of his actions all began at a single moment of temptation where David was not being careful.

One evening, while hanging around and doing nothing at his palace (similar to my dorm room temptation), David happened to see a beautiful young woman bathing on her roof. Once the fuse of his passion was lit (which often takes place visually for men), David had already sinned against God by lusting after her with his eyes and now was well on his way to sinning against God in greater ways.

David could have short-circuited the temptation by proactively planning something else to do on that lonely night at the palace. David could have turned the other way once he saw the great looking woman on her roof, invoking Job's words that *"I made a covenant with my eyes not to look lustfully at a girl"* (Job 31:1). David didn't have to have his servants invite her up to his room. As is the case with our temptations, at many points in the story God provided a way out of all of David's bad choices. Our temptations are nothing new. They are not unique to our generation, and God's promises to provide ways out are as true today as they were thousands of years ago. The responsibility of looking for that way out is ours.

IN HIS OWN WORDS
Chris, University of Virginia Graduate
Charlottesville, Virginia

I was raised in an upper middle class family that was nominally Christian. Christmas and Easter – maybe. I was basically a pretty good kid, never getting in too much trouble. High school athletics became a large part of my experience and a good friend on my football team introduced me to Christianity. Not nominal religiosity, but a Christianity that marked, shaped and formed his life. Growing up, I had never not believed in God, but I had also never clearly understood that I was a sinner in need of forgiveness and soul-rescue through Christ.

I received Christ as my Lord and Savior in high school, where being a Christian was (this seems odd to me now) a very popular thing. There were no real challenges to my new faith. I enjoyed continued success in athletics and accepted a football scholarship to an Atlantic Coast Conference school, the University of Virginia. Very soon I realized I was "not in Kansas anymore."

I left my high school cocoon and naively allowed myself to become isolated and alone. Not in a clinically depressed way, but in the sense that I was not known as a Christian to my new acquaintances in my new college world. And the newer, bigger, more exciting, looser college culture was anonymous and interesting.

As a college athlete it was easy to be put or be welcomed into compromising situations. Honestly, while I intellectually knew there were moral, physical and spiritual dangers ahead, I neither prized nor wanted accountability that comes from close friendships with fellow believers. As a result, I did things freely and foolishly that assaulted my faith, weakened my convictions, disoriented my moral compass, and hurt others.

I am certain that had I maintained my public profession and sought-out like minded believers, I would have been held accountable. I would have been challenged against going in sinful and dangerous directions. I was like a single stranded rope that easily breaks – weak in my isolation, exposed to temptation, and kept foolish apart from the wise counsel of others.

While I wasn't overtly arrogant, strutting around toting a football while wearing my letter jacket, I seriously overestimated my own ability to discern right from wrong and to do the right things. Why would someone in his right mind, concerned generally for his own self preservation and well being, willingly become detached from sources of spiritual and moral support? Simple answer: Pride. I had sadly over-estimated my own moral fiber and spiritual strength, and because I was isolated I couldn't be helped and strengthened by other Christians.

At times I was on the path, but was dissatisfied and wanted to try other things (by-paths). Other times, I rambled boldly and proudly off the path in my own directions. It is a serious thing to be discontent with the wise and good paths God sets before us. But, it is fool-hearty and destructive to toy with leaving the way, or to willingly charge into the deep woods.

His Word urges us to cultivate and enjoy fellowship with other believers. It warns us that pride has brought and will continue to bring good people down (sometimes devastatingly). And, His Word is a light for our feet and a lamp as we walk His paths for us. Commitment to holiness and purity is an investment of immense value.

"Mistakes will happen," some say. While this is true, some mistakes are inconsequential. Others, however, can have very serious consequences, leaving lasting bitter images, unpleasant memories, psychological wounds and emotional scars. College students should realize that they, and those with whom they may be involved, will carry these effects into all their future relationships – most importantly, into their marriages.

Now that I'm a father, my prayer for my own children is that they will be kept in the way and in the Word, and thereby avoid the serious consequences of sinful choices. I challenge students with *Galatians 6:7-9*:

Do not be deceived: God cannot be mocked. A man reaps what he sows. The one who sows to please his sinful nature, from that nature will reap destruction; the one who sows to please the Spirit, from the Spirit will reap eternal life. Let us not become weary in doing good, for at the proper time we will reap a harvest if we do not give up.

Reflecting the Character of Christ

Two things are required for success in combating temptation on the college campus, and King David's struggles are great pictures for us. First, we are told to be careful when we think we are standing firm. We have to know our limitations. Humility must be the overarching characteristic of our lives: humility regarding just how spiritually immature we are, humility about how susceptible we are to all sorts of temptation, and humility about how weak we are going to be in certain situations and with certain people. Humility is a unique characteristic in our culture of self-help, self-improvement, and self-promotion. Do you genuinely want to have people recognize Christ in you? Try making humility your crowning characteristic.

The great Baptist preacher and author, Charles H. Spurgeon, wrote about Jesus:

See the master taking a towel and washing His disciples' feet! Follower of Christ, wilt thou not humble thyself? See Him as the servant of servants, and surely thou canst not be proud! Is not this sentence the compendium of His biography, 'He humbled Himself' (Philippians 2:8)?

Was He not on earth always stripping off first one robe of honour and then another, till, naked, He was fastened to the cross, and there did He not empty out His inmost self, pouring out His life-blood, giving up for all of us, till they laid Him penniless in a borrowed grave? How low was our dear Redeemer brought! How then can we be proud?[3]

My freshman year in school I zealously avoided drinking alcohol. While that was wise for me, my demeanor about my abstinence was self-righteous and often offensive to friends in my dorm. When asked why I didn't drink, I would pompously respond along the lines of "It is morally wrong, unholy, and I want to obey the Lord our God!" Understandably, people found that disingenuous, and they were correct. Sensing their offense, I began to take stock of my approach and, during my second year of college, I took a different tack.

From that point on, when asked why I wasn't drinking, I humbly answered, "I'm not able to drink without getting drunk. I'm a terrible drunk who cannot handle my liquor. I'm going to end up places I don't want to end up and more than likely hurt myself and others in the process. I'm a screwed up, broken person." The response of my dorm-mates after that was incredibly supportive, and they often stepped in when others would try to make me feel awkward about not partying. They would say, "Hey, didn't you hear him—he can't handle it. Leave him alone."

---

[3] Spurgeon, Charles H., *Morning and Evening* (Henderson Publishers, 1991), pg. 311.

It was an amazing turnabout for me, and I learned an important lesson. My first response to inquiries about my sobriety was filled with self-righteous claims of superiority, which are dishonest at their heart. In my natural state, I did not really want to obey the Lord. Apart from His grace working in me on a daily basis, I would be as inclined as King David to stray from God's commands. When I started answering with true humility, made possible by the security I have in Christ who saved me, not because of righteous things I had done but because of His mercy (*Titus 3:5*), people were surprised.

I was also asked from time to time, "If you know you're so broken and weak, how do you feel okay about yourself and go to church so much?" That was always my favorite question, as it generally led to an opportunity to share the gospel; that it is Christ's complete righteousness that makes us acceptable to the Father and not our own perfection. As it says in *Romans 3:20-22*:

> *No one will be declared righteous in his sight by observing the law, rather through the law we become conscious of sin. But now a righteousness from God, apart from law, has been made known, to which the Law and the Prophets testify. This righteousness from God comes through faith in Jesus Christ to all who believe.*

Humility is the first step to successfully overcoming temptation. The absence of pride will make us realize we can't go it alone (Tip #1) and make us careful about where we go and with whom we will go. The second component of overcoming temptation is appropriating wisdom in our decisions about what we do and when we do it. This wisdom is appropriated as we interact with Jesus on a personal basis.

The Christian life isn't just about avoiding going to hell. God has prescribed in His Word a plan for us that encourages intimacy with Him through the presence of His Holy Spirit. Christian living isn't about "doing right and avoiding wrong;" it is about knowing the presence of the God and seeking to honor and please Him in our every day lives.

Spiritual growth is about growing in our experience with Jesus, not simply our knowledge of theology or our experiences in worship. Maturity in Christ is learning to practice the presence of God and making choices each day that His Word says will bring Him joy instead of grief. And yes, the Holy Spirit is a person who can be grieved by our bad decision making (see *Ephesians 4:30*). The great promise from *Psalm 23:4* is that, even though we walk through the valley of the shadow of death, God is there with us. This promise is comforting during times of distress. However, if you're of the mind to disobey God's commands, His ongoing presence will absolutely ruin your "good time."

When I started wandering into territory that I knew was morally out of bounds, I always had to purposefully attempt to push thoughts of the Lord out my mind. I can say from experience that this is a futile exercise for a Christian who wants to maintain intimacy with God. When we try to ignore the Lord through our disobedience, the grieved Holy Spirit brings a conviction that causes godly sorrow and, ultimately, repentance.

The long and short of it is that, one way or another, a child of God will have to kneel at the feet of their heavenly Father. The choice is whether we're going to do that in advance so we can appropriate His strength and experience His joy, or whether we do that on the back side of falling to temptation and experience the sorrow of disappointing and grieving a Savior who died for us.

Some live their lives by the credo that it's easier to get forgiveness than permission, so they do what they want to and apologize later if necessary. Not only is this a poor human relationships strategy, I've known some who had that attitude toward God. My experience has taught me that it is highly preferable to seek intimacy for overcoming temptation rather than for forgiveness for rebellion. If someone is a real Christian, intimacy with God is a certainty; it's just a matter of when and how.

The "Way Out There" Way Out

Teri was a gorgeous young Christian woman from my hometown who I went out with a few times during the winter break of my sophomore year. We enjoyed each others company, laughed at each others jokes, and thought each other physically attractive. Unfortunately, Teri and I got fooling around on those first couple of dates, crossing a moral boundary or two.

While we didn't go as far as we could have, we still went far beyond our professed standards and our desire to please the Lord. That next summer, I was going to be home for only one week, and we agreed that we would spend some time together then. I had a few months to battle the temptation and to think about what we could possibly do once we got together. I battled those temptations, by God's grace and strength, taking my thoughts captive as often as possible.

Summer arrived and my time with Teri was upon me. We went to dinner, then to a movie. Afterward I made a tactical error when I asked her if she wanted to go for a walk in the park at night. What I knew as we exited my car and began to stroll deep into the park was that no one was around. I realized then what I am articulating here: that this was a one-step violation of my own first two survival Tips. Teri and I sat down on a bridge that covered a creek and made casual conversation for a while.

After a time of being in the middle of nowhere with this beautiful young Christian woman with whom I had previously been sexually involved, I began to sense the onset of temptation. Like the tractor beam that pulls the small spacecraft into the science fiction space station, I was feeling pulled in by the powerful force of physical attraction and sexual tension.

At the moment of greatest temptation—and in spite of the fact that I had foolishly walked headlong into this situation—God quietly nudged my heart with the thought that I had spent months trying to discipline my thoughts and this was the moment of truth. At that moment, I began to look for the way out. What I came up with—or what God provided, depending on how you look at it—makes me laugh to this day and makes me wonder why Teri ever talked to me again.

As I leaned in to kiss her, I stopped. I bowed my head and prayed very loudly, "Lord, help! I know I've done a poor job of leading this date tonight but I don't want to blow it. I don't want to dishonor your daughter here and I don't want to displease you. So help, please." I knew this was an odd thing to do before kissing a girl, but I was desperate not to screw up this date as I had so many dates before. To my delight, I heard Teri begin to pray along with me. After a few minutes of thanking the Lord for His grace, His goodness, His mercy, His kindness, and His presence, we concluded our time of prayer and talked about all things spiritual.

With great joy, I drove her home and we parted company, having shared only the affectionate hug of two friends who battled temptation together and survived. As I made my way back to my parents' house, the joy of God's presence was so palpable that I sang songs of praise to Him. It was one of the most significant spiritual moments of my life. It was possible because God was faithful to not allow me to be tempted beyond my ability to remain firm, and He kept His promise to provide a way out of the temptation.

I refer to that event as my "'Way Out There' Way Out," because of how nuts it seemed to me at the time. But I'll take the genuine joy of pleasing the Lord any day over the temporary sensation of pleasing my flesh. That is ultimately what fuels our obedience: the knowledge of His grace, and a response of gratitude that demonstrates a desire to love God through our obedience.

Jesus said in *John 14:15-21*:

"If you love me, you will obey what I command. And I will ask the Father, and he will give you another Counselor to be with you forever—the Spirit of truth. The world cannot accept him, because it neither sees him nor knows him. But you know him, for he lives with you and will be in you. I will not leave you as orphans; I will come to

you. Before long, the world will not see me anymore, but you will see me. Because I live, you also will live. On that day you will realize that I am in my Father, and you are in me, and I am in you. Whoever has my commands and obeys them, he is the one who loves me. He who loves me will be loved by my Father, and I too will love him and show myself to him."

We do not earn or secure our status as God's children through our obedience, but if we want to please our God in our walk with Him, we will obey Him. The presence of His Holy Spirit is there to empower us and motivate us to follow the Word of God. Tip #1 is about keeping others around us who will remind us of the presence of God in our lives and stimulate us to love Him and worship Him. Tip #2 is about humbly recognizing His presence and power in our lives, knowing that we can do nothing without Him. That kind of humility will protect us, guide us, and help us safely negotiate the temptations of the college campus.

RANDOM TIP "C"
Be Proactive in Avoiding the Party Scene

I went to college at a well-known "party school," West Virginia University. But, I've heard of very few colleges (including Christian ones) that didn't have a significant party scene. Part and parcel of this party culture is rampant alcohol consumption. Binge drinking is a real problem at most colleges.

When you're in high school, assuming you had the desire to drink alcohol, it was most likely difficult to come by. As a teenager I had to expend significant energy and skills in deception in order to get drunk because (a) I was underage and couldn't buy alcohol; (b) I had very little money with which to buy it, and (c) I knew I had to go home to my parents at the end of the night.

Your first semester on campus you discover three things: (1) Rarely does anyone check your age; (2) there is free booze at lots of the parties, and (3) your parents are not there to oversee your behavior anymore. Needless to say, alcohol use and abuse becomes a problem for lots of college students.

If you struggle with abusing alcohol, as I did, you'll have to determine before you get to campus how you'll avoid putting yourself in situations that will tempt you to get drunk. For the record, it is illegal for you to consume alcoholic beverages in the United States if you're under the age of 21. Sorry to be the bad cop, but Romans 13:1 says we're obligated to obey the civil laws.

My point is that if you don't proactively search out fun things to do without alcohol, the party scene will come to you. Whether it's friends in your dorm, apartment complex or Greek brothers or sisters, there is always somebody looking for someone to party with them. I'm speaking from both personal experience and from watching students not get creative about what their social world looked like.

If you don't work to develop a lifestyle free from alcohol abuse, unlike high school you won't be able to avoid the partying because in college the party will come to your front door. You have to be socially proactive or you will fall down, much like trying to remain stationary while sitting on a bicycle. To make it safely through college, you and your friends (see Tip #1) will have to put your heads together to find ways to enjoy yourselves while you avoid getting trapped in a social world that revolves around alcohol.

www.threetips.com

Tip #3: NEVER LEAVE THE PATH

Be Clear About What You Believe

Enter through the narrow gate. For wide is the gate and broad is the road that leads to destruction, and many enter through it. But small is the gate and narrow the road that leads to life, and only a few find it.
Matthew 17:3-4

If there is no resurrection of the dead, then not even Christ has been raised. And if Christ has not been raised, our preaching is useless and so is your faith. More than that, we are then found to be false witnesses about God, for we have testified about God that he raised Christ from the dead. But he did not raise him if in fact the dead are not raised. For if the dead are not raised, then Christ has not been raised either. And if Christ has not been raised, your faith is futile; you are still in your sins.
1 Corinthians 15:13-17

Jesus answered, "I am the way and the truth and the life. No one comes to the Father except through me. If you really knew me, you would know my Father as well. From now on, you do know him and have seen him." Philip said, "Lord, show us the Father and that will be enough for us."
Jesus answered: "Don't you know me, Philip, even after I have been among you such a long time? Anyone who has seen me has seen the Father.
John 14:6-9

"Give us clear vision that we may know where to stand and what to stand for - because unless we stand for something, we shall fall for anything."
Peter Marshall, U.S. Senate Chaplain 1947

Do As I Say, Not As I Do

As I've said on many occasions, I'm an expert at moral inability. If there's a way to screw up, I've found it. And that applies to the very rules I'm writing here, as witnessed in a recent experience.

While writing this book, I had the occasion to go hiking with my kids and their cousins in the mountains of northwest New Jersey. It is beautiful countryside and the forest where we were hiking had clearly marked paths.

Being the leader of the pack, I moved at a brisk pace and paid little attention to how closely or far behind the pack was trailing me. A good bit of time went by before I realized that the group had fallen behind or gone a different direction than I had. As I backtracked in an attempt to locate them, I violated Tip #3; I left the path.

As you might guess, it wasn't long before I was lost. I didn't know which way was north, south, east or west. I started to yell and whistle loudly in the hopes that someone from our group would hear me. Fortunately, as I continued to track through the woods, I heard voices in the distance and very quickly made my way toward them. It was my family. Did I tell them I got lost? Of course not. I acted as if I had instead gone off to investigate the wilderness on my own and skillfully found my way back to civilization. My wife knew differently.

"The Path" is often referred to as a morality path, or a set of rules that guide our behavior. "Staying on the narrow path" is a saying that has come to symbolize living a moral lifestyle. However, in New Testament terms, the narrow path is the means or method by which human beings are able to come and enjoy the benefits of being children of God.

Christianity has always contended that Jesus was God in the flesh, that he was punished for our sins so we wouldn't have to be, and that as we trust in Him as the atoning sacrifice for our sins, we are not held guilty for the wrongs we have done in this life. Furthermore, because Christians have the presence of God's Holy Spirit living in them, they have been transformed and appear as spotless as Jesus because the good works of the Son have been credited to the person who looks to the Father for salvation.

The ambition of this chapter is to help you get a firm grip on the nature of basic Christianity so you can distinguish the real God from the imitation. As you head off to campus, you will have friends and professors who will expose you to a myriad of other religions and ways of thinking. You'll discover things you never knew and couldn't even imagine. Sometimes,

Christian students are convinced that their "religion" is no different than any other world religion, and they have a difficult time answering questions about their faith.

In this situation, many students assume that the faith of their youth was imposed on them by their parents, pastors, or peers and they come to the conclusion that they don't believe any longer what they used to. In my experience, though, few of those students understood basic Christianity in the first place, and were unable to contrast the religions and philosophical systems they studied in college from the Christian faith of their youth. I believe that as you comprehend the nature of the Gospel (the word gospel means "good news"), it will enable you to fairly easily compare, contrast, and distinguish what you believe from other systems of thought.

Additionally, I've discovered that students who understood a few critical components about Christianity (i.e., who Jesus was, why He died, and that He arose from the dead), these students endure the intellectual challenges to their beliefs and actually find a renewed freedom and confidence to explore world religions and philosophy without a nagging sense that they're going to get confused or led astray. Unfortunately, leading students astray is a hobby for some.

Lessons from the Shunammite Woman

We saw in Tip #2 that staying on the right moral path requires humility, but it also presumes that a person has confidence that the narrow path is the best direction for them. For someone to stay on the path of Christ, they have to believe that He wouldn't require it of them if it weren't in their best interest. Jesus said that the narrow path was the one we should walk, because the wide path is the one that everyone else takes and it leads to destruction *(Matthew 17:3-4)*. The narrow path requires focus and concentration. It is a lot more work and is a lot lonelier than the path that everyone else is walking. Ultimately, a Christian student has to trust what God's Word says about which path to take, where the path is leading, and how to walk along it.

Another powerful Old Testament story is that of the Shunammite woman's experience with God and His servant Elisha found in *2 Kings*. Before I show you the relevant lesson from her encounter with God's Word in *2 Kings 8*, we need to first do the background on how she began her relationship with God's prophet, Elisha. In *2 Kings 4*, after befriending the prophet, she is blessed by God to give birth to a son. One day when working with his father in the fields, her son developed a head injury that led to his death. Knowing that God's prophet was her friend, the Shunammite woman called for Elisha to come and care for her son. 2 *Kings 4:32-37* picks up the story when Elisha arrives at the home.

When Elisha reached the house, there was the boy lying dead on his couch. He went in, shut the door on the two of them and prayed to the LORD. Then he got on the bed and lay upon the boy, mouth to mouth, eyes to eyes, hands to hands. As he stretched himself out upon him, the boy's body grew warm. Elisha turned away and walked back and forth in the room and then got on the bed and stretched out upon him once more. The boy sneezed seven times and opened his eyes. Elisha summoned Gehazi and said, "Call the Shunammite." And he did. When she came, he said, "Take your son." She came in, fell at his feet and bowed to the ground. Then she took her son and went out.

It occurs to me as I read this what a strange scene this must have been: the kid wakes up to find a man laying on top of him, and the prophet is wiping snot off his face and wondering why God couldn't have just healed the kid when he knelt down to pray for him the first time.

In any case, the kid came back to life and Elisha once again showed God's graciousness and love for this Shunammite woman. It is against that background that her 2 *Kings 8* encounter must be read. A famine is coming on the land and Elisha knows this. He passes along this inside info to his friend, and instructs her to do something that requires great trust in him. She is able to listen to him and follow those instructions because of her previous encounters with God's grace through Elisha. Read this account from *2 Kings 8:*

Now Elisha had said to the woman whose son he had restored to life, "Go away with your family and stay for a while wherever you can, because the LORD has decreed a famine in the land that will last seven years." The woman proceeded to do as the man of God said. She and her family went away and stayed in the land of the Philistines seven years.

At the end of the seven years she came back from the land of the Philistines and went to the king to beg for her house and land. The king was talking to Gehazi, the servant of the man of God, and had said, "Tell me about all the great things Elisha has done." Just as Gehazi was telling the king how Elisha had restored the dead to life, the woman whose son Elisha had brought back to life came to beg the king for her house and land.

Gehazi said, "This is the woman, my lord the king, and this is her son whom Elisha restored to life." The king asked the woman about it, and she told him. Then he assigned an official to her case and said to him, "Give back everything that belonged to her, including all the income from her land from the day she left the country until now."

The first difficult challenge associated with following the prophet's instruction was to leave her home and live for several years living among foreigners who often were hostile to Jews. Secondly, by leaving her land unattended for that long, she was essentially giving up her claim to the property. By listening to

Elisha, she and her family were going to be alone and have to sacrifice one of the biggest assets they owned: their land.

After seven years she "happens" back onto the scene at the exact moment when Elisha's assistant, Gehazi, was telling Israel's king about Elisha's greatest hits, the greatest being when he lay on top of this kid and brought him back to life. Then he turns and sees the very Shunammite woman about whom he was talking. It must have put quite a point on the story. After the king hears the story, he does two amazing things that give us a beautiful picture of the grace of God.

Once the King establishes that the Shunammite woman's relationship with Elisha is legitimate, he determines to give the family land back to her. But it isn't simply that she gets the land, he gives her the sum total of all the money that the family would've made during their absence. And here's the kicker: if she had stayed during the famine years in disobedience to the prophet, there is a good chance the family would've starved to death. Even if they had survived, it's certain that they wouldn't have made any money farming the land because they wouldn't have been able to grow any crops.

Let's review: a woman has an encounter with God's kindness that enables her to trust the Word of the Lord when she's instructed to leave her land and move to a foreign country for several years. In response to her trust in Him, God blesses the woman once again upon her return through her relationship with Elisha. Through this association she is given not only what was hers to begin with, but that which was never hers—that which she could never have earned by her own efforts. This is the gospel of Jesus Christ. Because of our association with Jesus, our Father and King graciously gives us a reward that we in our moral inability could never have earned on our own.

Grace is not about avoiding the punishment you deserve, but getting the reward you don't deserve. In Christ, we are not only forgiven for our sins through his willingness to be punished for our sins, but we are credited with his good works and that gives us access to all of His blessings. We are now given that which we don't deserve and all because of our relationship with Jesus.

As for staying on the path, where you and I have to begin is by being clear about our initial encounter with Jesus. He loves us first, and then we love Him in response. He saved us, not because of any good thing we've done but just because of his mercy (see *Titus 3:5-6*). God is gracious and wants us to know and experience a relationship with Him. However, this relationship is based solely on His willingness to forgive us of our sins and credit us with the righteousness (good works) of

Christ. Seeing and experiencing God's grace in Christ is a must if you ever expect to be able to trust Him enough to stay on the path when it is so tempting to venture off on your own way.

God wants to bless our obedience by providing more for us if we obey Him than if we tried to figure out how to live life on our own, through our instincts, or by following the wide path that everyone else is following to destruction. This is the essence of staying on the path morally.

But the starting point for walking the path is first understanding the path theologically. If you are not clear about why you are OK with God, then it is unlikely that you will be able to obey God when He calls you to walk the narrow path. It's also unlikely that you will be able to discern when someone tries to convince you that your path is either the wrong one or one of a myriad of correct paths.

This is where many get tripped up during college. A fellow student or professor introduces new and thought-provoking questions and propositions about religion, and the new information causes confusion and sometimes significant doubt about the reliability of the information that a young Christian was taught by parents, pastors, or peers before coming to college.

We could classify all the religions in the world in one of three categories. The first system is one whereby through religion one strives to become a better person. We perform good works for others and follow whatever rules or creeds are part of whatever religious system we're part of, all in an effort to earn or merit God's blessings either in this life or the next. Most every religion is some form of this equation:

Our Good Works = Our Salvation

The second religious system is one by which God exists, mankind is fallible and incapable of being perfect, but God intends on forgiving everyone. It is often referred to as "Universalism" because God intends on saving everyone in the universe regardless of their moral performance on this planet or what they believe about Him. You can think of this religious system in terms of this equation:

Our Existence = Our Salvation

The third system is what Jesus came to do. Perfection is demanded of us if we're to be in the holy presence of God and justice is demanded for sins committed against Him. All of mankind is sinful and deserves to be condemned eternally for their evil heart and deeds, regardless of how much better or worse they deem themselves compared to others.

Because none of us are perfect and we have no means of satisfying the just demands of a holy God, our Heavenly Father sent Jesus Christ, His only begotten Son (who is also God in His being) to do two things: First, Jesus was to be punished for the sins of everyone who would ever put their trust in Him so God's justice could be satisfied. Jesus was perfect (he was deity) so His life could be substituted for ours, the righteous for the unrighteous (*1 Peter 3:18*).

Secondly, through His sinless, perfect life Jesus Christ would earn for us the requirement to be in the presence of God and give those who trust Him credit for His good works. System three can best be represented by this equation:

Reliance on the Work of Christ Alone = Our Salvation

There are significant differences between system three (historic Christianity) and the first two. In the first system, assuming that one could live a "good enough" life to avoid making any big blunders or overtly hurting anyone, perfection isn't possible, so there is no way of knowing until the dreaded "Judgment Day" as to whether or not a person is OK with God.

Even assuming one could perform ably enough the religious duties prescribed for them, they ultimately would be the one credited with their salvation. A person in this system inevitably falls prey to self-righteousness. In their pride they will credit themselves with enough goodness and well-intentioned behavior to essentially force God's hand to allow them into His presence or obligate God to allow their safe passage into a pleasant afterlife. Mankind is the center of this religion and the one who receives the credit for the good works.

In system two, regardless of what it is called, mankind can act unjustly and there is no eternal system of justice or punishment—regardless of how cruel, evil, or horrifying the behavior on this earth. The monsters of history, from the Roman Emperor Nero to Attila the Hun to Genghis Khan to Adolph Hitler and everyone before and after them, are all free from any divine justice. God, if He exists at all, will simply look the other way and say "I forgive you." There is no requirement of faith or good works or acknowledgment of any of our wrongdoings. In this system God, if He exists, is unjust.

Only in the person of Jesus Christ is this dilemma of mercy and justice solved. The apostle Paul wrote that, through

Jesus Christ, God is able to be just (Jesus satisfies His holy requirement for the punishment of sins) and able to be merciful (we are spared the punishment we deserve). The good news of the gospel is clearly summarized in *Romans 3:20-26*:

Therefore no one will be declared righteous in his sight by observing the law; rather, through the law we become conscious of sin. But now a righteousness from God, apart from law, has been made known, to which the Law and the Prophets testify. This righteousness from God comes through faith in Jesus Christ to all who believe. There is no difference, for all have sinned and fall short of the glory of God, and are justified freely by his grace through the redemption that came by Christ Jesus.

God presented him as a sacrifice of atonement through faith in his blood. He did this to demonstrate his justice, because in his forbearance he had left the sins committed beforehand unpunished — he did it to demonstrate his justice at the present time, so as to be just and the one who justifies those who have faith in Jesus.

Carrie's Story

Carrie came to Christ through the influence of her family and started attending the youth group where I was the Pastor to Students. She seemed to thrive in our ministry and was one of the super intelligent kids in the group. As a high school student she excelled academically and got an academic scholarship to college. During her senior year of high school she appeared to be progressing well spiritually, as she often attended events at the university with older and more mature Christians. As she headed off to college, her spiritual future seemed very bright.

Then she fell off the proverbial map. No visiting our church when she was home. No emails or correspondence from school. During her first summer break at home, she avoided our college group. We finally had a chance to visit about what was going on in her life, and she informed me that she didn't believe any longer what she claimed to believe when she was in high school. She had attended a class where she read materials that supposedly proved to her that the Bible wasn't reliable.

Being the logical and intelligent woman that she was, she knew that once you take away the source of inspiration and "truth," you're not left with much but speculation. She correctly surmised that if the Bible was not God's authoritative Word, you couldn't know whether Jesus Christ actually said all the things he was reported in the Gospels to have said.

Additionally, if Jesus wasn't really who the Scriptures described Him to be—God incarnate—then in Christ you really didn't have an "in the flesh" picture of the character and personality of God. Carrie took a significant theological turn, abandoning the Scriptures as a source of authoritative truth and the belief that Jesus Christ was God in human flesh and Savior of the world's sinners. She instead began a quest to find truth in other ways. I sent her some materials in an attempt to reignite her trust in the Scriptures, but didn't get a response. Her mind was made up. In her thinking, greater minds had already pointed her in the right direction.

I remember the "greater" minds of the religion department of my undergraduate years. These were the professors who condescendingly tolerated people who believed in the supernatural. These "intelligent" instructors thought foolish the silly Christian kids who presupposed that if an all-powerful God existed that He could do whatever He wanted.

During my junior year at WVU, my friend Dave (who was really smart and became a physician) and I (who was not very smart and became a disc-jockey) took an Old Testament class. As two enthusiastic, young, Christian men, we thought this would encourage our faith as we dug into the major themes of certain books of Holy Writ. We were shocked at just how different the experience was. Our professor was very clear from the start that while he was an expert in the contents of the Old Testament, he was not a believer in their inspiration or inerrancy.

On top of that, he "allegorized" most of the 39 books of the Old Testament, meaning that he didn't believe that most of the events actually happened. The way he saw it, these stories were handed down orally and therefore these oral histories couldn't be trusted. He, as have others, liken oral history to the game of "telephone," where you tell someone next to you a secret and they pass it around the circle to several friends until it comes back to you completely different from how it started.

This is a weak argument because it assumes that these Old Testament "oral" histories weren't told out loud. The argument presumes that oral histories weren't communicated in groups where others could verify the accuracy of the details, and that nothing was ever written down. In fact, tribes that pre-date the Israelites wrote things down on tablets and painted their histories on walls.

But our professor didn't want to hear this either. He contended that Moses didn't write down the history of the Israel at all, that others did so and ascribed the authorship to Moses. Through a series of complex arguments that were barely comprehensible to undergraduate students, he tried to prove to us that Moses couldn't have written these books. We weren't buying his arguments and he got increasingly frustrated with the two Christians in the class.

The problem was that whenever we pushed him to the sources of his argument, we discovered that he was completely relying on the scholarship of another person as the bedrock of what he believed. Information that was researched by one person a hundred years ago, elaborated on by another group of researchers who put together a text book (all with human agendas and fallibility), and then taught to our professor by another professor with his own biases. Then it is finally delivered to us in the classroom by our professor.

When asked if he had ever studied the original research, our Professor replied that time prohibited him from doing so and that the academic checks and balances are so effective that he had to "trust" them. Sounds like the game "telephone," doesn't it?

When our class studied the book of Jonah, he laughed at us when we asserted that we thought that Jonah being swallowed alive by a big fish was a real, historical event. Why did he laugh? Because he had reasoned that other cultures had similar myths, that Israel's history was unenlightened compared to ours just like every other ancient civilization, and that it is scientifically impossible for a man to have lived inside the belly of a big fish for three days and then be coughed up onto the beach still alive.

My religion professor and I were working from a different set of presuppositions regarding Jonah. His were:

A) It was scientifically impossible and a violation of natural law for Jonah to be able to live inside the belly of a large fish for three days.

B) Ancient literature is filled with myths and allegories that explain natural phenomenon using super-natural fictions.

C) The Israelite people were no different than any other group that lived 1000-2000 years before Jesus Christ.

D) The Jews created myths to try and explain their history and the God they believed in.

E) Jonah's experience, as recorded in the Old Testament, was an allegory and not an actual historical event.

Compare these to my set of presuppositions:

A) God exists and because of the sheer size and complexity of the universe we can intelligently surmise that He is powerful and is able to do whatever He desires.

B) Jesus Christ, after being bodily resurrected from the dead, verified the New Testament claim that He is God incarnate, deity veiled in flesh, the one through whom all things were created.

C) Because Jesus Christ's resurrection from death was impossible naturally, God clearly overrides His own natural laws when He wants to.

D) In *Matthew 12:40*, Jesus compared his own physical resurrection from the dead after three days to that of Jonah's three days in the belly of a huge fish.

E) Jonah's experience, as recorded in the Old Testament, was an actual historical event.

One's presuppositions don't make them a bad person, or unintelligent, but they will ultimately cause them to form a different set of conclusions. The same occurs when a "Bible believing" person processes a lot of what gets presented as scientific fact. If Scripture is clear that something happened a certain way, but the laws of natural science say that it couldn't possibly have happened that way, that doesn't mean either the scientist is evil or the believer is an idiot.

Christians intelligently presuppose the existence of a powerful, supernatural God, and that affects our willingness to believe that the miraculous can and does happen. It doesn't surprise me that from time to time my profession of faith runs counter to the naturalistic presuppositions of others.

It is also important to point out that not every Bible believer has the same understanding of what Scripture is teaching, and therefore potentially has a different methodology for processing scientific data. There are Christians who are faithful to Scripture who don't believe that it teaches that God created the world in six, 24-hour days. The "Day Age" and "Framework" interpretations of the Genesis creation account are widely accepted as faithful to Scripture, which is the real issue at hand regarding a Christian world-view.

The mantra of the Protestant Reformation was *Sola Scriptura*, which means "Scripture Alone." The Christian must be committed first to the teaching of the Scriptures, the special revelation of God to man. That doesn't mean the general revelation that we discover about our world doesn't play a role in the formation of our worldview. It simply means that when Scripture (special revelation) and nature (general revelation) contradict one another, Scripture and the teaching it contains prevail in what we believe.

That may seem problematic to many because it potentially puts our belief system at odds with those who don't presuppose the existence of God and the deity of Jesus. This tension is nothing new, as the professed beliefs of Christianity were often a cause for execution up until the third century, A.D. Also, Jesus warned His disciples that believing in Him would at times put them (and us) at odds with the people of our world. Here's what he said in *John 15:18-25*:

> *"If the world hates you, keep in mind that it hated me first. If you belonged to the world, it would love you as its own. As it is, you do not belong to the world, but I have chosen you out of the world. That is why the world hates you. Remember the words I spoke to you: 'No servant is greater than his master.' If they persecuted me, they will persecute you also. If they obeyed my teaching, they will obey yours also. They will treat you this way because of my name, for they do not*

know the One who sent me. If I had not come and spoken to them, they would not be guilty of sin. Now, however, they have no excuse for their sin. He who hates me hates my Father as well. If I had not done among them what no one else did, they would not be guilty of sin. But now they have seen these miracles, and yet they have hated both me and my Father. But this is to fulfill what is written in their Law: 'They hated me without reason.'"

Having a different understanding of the world doesn't make you stupid, but there are always going to be people who try to make you feel that way for believing that Jesus is who Scripture teaches Him to be. Most mean well, they are simply working from an entirely different set of preconceived ideas and beliefs. Your beliefs may, from time to time, put you at odds with the way others understand the world around them. The commitment to which Jesus calls Christians is to love others and to be respectful toward them regardless of whether they agree with you or treat you kindly.

I've been embarrassed by the conduct of some (and myself as I think back to my studies) as they interact with hostility toward their professors and others who disagree with them. There is no room for the Christian to behave in such a way. We are to be winsome in our demeanor, humble in our character, and loving in our actions. The angry and frustrated religious person who can't allow for others to think differently or see the world differently does nothing to convince others that they should reconsider their way of seeing the world.

So relax. Jesus is alive. He is God. He has, can, and will do whatever He wants to in order to bring about the world which He created. Obey Him and love others with all of your heart. When they mock you, love them. When they belittle you, love them. When they condescend to you about what you've pre-committed to thinking in your "cute little belief system," love them. And take heart because Jesus is alive.

When the chief priests had met with the elders and devised a plan, they gave the soldiers a large sum of money, telling them, "You are to say, 'His disciples came during the night and stole him away while we were asleep.' If this report gets to the governor, we will satisfy him and keep you out of trouble." So the soldiers took the money and did as they were instructed. And this story has been widely circulated among the Jews to this very day.

Then the eleven disciples went to Galilee, to the mountain where Jesus had told them to go. When they saw him, they worshiped him; but some doubted. Then Jesus came to them and said, "All authority in heaven and on earth has been given to me. Therefore go and make disciples of all nations, baptizing them in the name of the Father and of the Son and of the Holy Spirit, and teaching them to obey everything I have commanded you. And surely I am with you always, to the very end of the age."
Matthew 28:12-20

IN HIS OWN WORDS
James, West Virginia University Graduate
Morgantown, West Virginia

I grew up in a Christian home and attended a Bible-believing church. My Father was the pastor and my mother a stay-at-home mom. My parents were devoted to the church and to raising me and my sister in the "fear and admonition of the Lord." We had good Sunday school teachers, were involved in all of the youth programs as we got older, and thrived in this secure environment. But none of this prepared me for what I would face when I got out of a Christian education environment.

My sophomore year of college, I was exposed to teachers that were committed to debunking Christianity and so-called "unenlightened" Christian ideas. They were good communicators and engaging teachers. Most of the students liked them, including me. But I found that, over the course of that year and the ones to follow, many of the views they suggested or advocated in class slowly eroded my confidence in the Bible and even God's existence.

I recall some of the arguments that brought me to question my Christian upbringing. Statements like "Christianity was spread by the sword like most other religions in the world;" "evolutionary science suggests that the Bible is fiction;" and "there are many profitable writings that have morphed into holy books over the centuries."

These objections were unnerving and made me feel insecure about what I believed. This feeling of disorientation led to an underlying fear about my future and about life in general. I didn't dare question my professors—mostly because I didn't know how to.

By the time I graduated from school, I was thoroughly confused and in doubt about the Christian faith I had been taught by my parents. I would spend the next four years in this state of agnosticism—not knowing if there was a God or if there was such a thing as truth, but secretly hoping that there was.

Fast forward to today and now I am a Bible teacher in a Christian school. In no way do I resemble the confused student of yesteryear. Looking back, it is hard to believe that such superficial statements could cause life-changing doubt in my faith. But they did, and if you're not prepared for these encounters, they'll create many of the same feelings in you.

My problem was that I did not have an argument to disprove the objections to my faith. In fact, I did not even have enough maturity to know that religious perspectives existed that were in conflict with mine. I had come face to face with differing viewpoints and was dumbfounded that anyone believed differently from me.

The modern pursuit of academic understanding requires that you question your beliefs. My parents never really questioned their basic assumptions about God and Christianity. As a result, they had no good defense for their faith nor did they train me where to turn when I was confused. I was defenseless and academia kicked my butt for a few years.

It is clear that such uninformed thinking may have worked in the past, but is woefully insufficient if a Christian is to survive in today's campus academic environment. For college football fans, the old saying goes, "Defense wins championships." Although a good offense is indispensable, rarely, if ever, does a team win a championship without a good defensive strategy.

For the Christian, that means knowing why our faith is true and knowing how to defend it. Satan is an untiring enemy who seeks to destroy our faith in God. Now more than ever, we must be equipped and prepared if we want to survive the college campus. One of my favorite verses is what the Apostle Paul said to a young Christian man named Timothy, in *1 Timothy 6:20-21:*

Timothy, guard what has been entrusted to your care. Turn away from godless chatter and the opposing ideas of what is falsely called knowledge, which some have professed and in so doing have wandered from the faith.

Some Thoughts about the Thinkers

I've had the privilege of both teaching Christian college students and watching Christians on both the college campus and in the classroom. Before I give you a few thoughts about the academic climate for Christians at many universities, there are some preliminary things I need to say. First of all, the professors who teach your classes are generally intelligent and learned and they have usually forgotten more about their topics than you know. Hence, you ought to approach them with the humility that recognizes that fact. Also, it would be helpful if you presume that they don't have a problem with your belief systems, because many do not.

Additionally, most of these professors are familiar with Christianity, particularly the professors in your religion department. More than likely you won't be sharing with them anything they don't already know. Thus, perhaps you ought to wait for them to inquire about your beliefs before you are perceived as arrogantly "introducing" to your teachers that which they already understand. As we'll get to later in this chapter, faith in Jesus is a spiritual encounter that requires the work of God's Holy Spirit.

So, if you want your professor to know the love of Christ, why not show it to them by being deferential to them and praying that they would see His love in you. Attending class, listening well and excelling academically would also go a long way toward impressing them. Also, pray that their colleagues who have a relationship with Jesus would be able to open a dialog about what it means to enjoy a relationship with God.

Regarding your religion department, you need to understand going into those classes that most of your professors aren't studying the Bible to "grow spiritually" as you and I do. They are studying religion and all of its sociological implications, as well as the historical significance of both Judaism and Christianity on the world around them. As a result, don't sign up for a religion class and then be surprised that they are challenging your previously held beliefs, as that is part of their job.

My religion professors at Florida State were very respectful to me, even as I knew that they didn't embrace the totality of my belief system. I was continually humbled by their graciousness toward me and by the sheer breadth of their knowledge of the subject matter. In that case, my experience was incredible and I left with a greater understanding of academic methodology and history.

That said, in many instances (including my undergraduate studies at WVU) the academic approach of some teaching at the college level is a condescending attempt to dismantle what you believe and then reassemble life in the manner in which the "all wise" professor wants you to see the world. Not all teachers are this way, and very few of my graduate professors at Florida State were like this toward me. But my friends who work as professors in the university system share stories with me about their colleagues' blatant hostility toward Christianity.

Most college Professors would deny this hostility toward "supernaturalists," a term used to describe people who presuppose that God has the power to override His own natural laws if desired. But in the politically sensitive culture of the university campus, even "crazy" Christians are protected from outright bias. Even if a professor felt negatively toward Christianity privately, they would not come right out and say, "I think Christians who believe that the Bible is trustworthy, that God 'created' the world and that mankind was the specific object of that creation, and that a human being named Jesus came back to life after being dead three days...well, they are all idiots."

But many Christian graduate students at the churches where I have been a pastor have said privately that it is socially challenging for them to be professing "Bible believers" in their respective departments. Higher education has its own set of presuppositions and evangelical Christians sometimes believe things that run counter to that set of underlying academic laws. At the top of that list of presuppositions is the notion that truth can be discovered through academic inquiry. But the Christian assumes even more fundamentally that natural man is not objective at all, and that his view of the world is terribly distorted by sin.

Romans 1:20-25 states:

For since the creation of the world God's invisible qualities—his eternal power and divine nature—have been clearly seen, being understood from what has been made, so that men are without excuse.
For although they knew God, they neither glorified him as God nor gave thanks to him, but their thinking became futile and their foolish hearts were darkened. Although they claimed to be wise, they became fools and exchanged the glory of the immortal God for images made to look like mortal man and birds and animals and reptiles.
Therefore God gave them over in the sinful desires of their hearts to sexual impurity for the degrading of their bodies with one another. They exchanged the truth of God for a lie, and worshiped and served created things rather than the Creator—who is forever praised. Amen.

Scripture teaches that our all-powerful God created the universe "ex nihilo" or out of nothing. Matter didn't exist eternally, waiting for the right combination of elements to mix and create a force that would be a catalyst for the creation of the world. God has existed eternally and as the Great Designer and

"First Cause" of all motion; He initiated the creation of the world. And yes, it made a big, huge bang!

The Scriptures say that it is foolishness to think that, apart from the power of God and His creative genius, that a cataclysmic explosion in space is what created a beautiful world with beings that are more intricately designed than the most expensive computer mankind could develop. *Psalm 14:1* says *"The fool says in his heart, 'There is no God.'"* But more than that, a fool will try to pacify those who are unwilling to listen or argue with those who disconnect themselves from the logic of what an all-powerful God could do. Could an all-powerful God create the world in six, 24-hour periods if He wanted to? Obviously, yes.

I'm not suggesting that it is unequivocally clear from Scripture that God did create the world in six literal days; I'm just asking whether or not an omnipotent God could do this if He wanted to. Could an all-powerful God keep a man alive in the belly of a large fish if He wanted to? Could the being who created the universe and placed each start in its specific orbit resurrect a man from the dead if He wanted to? Of course He could. That is, if He exists.

The Resurrection Apologetic

Regardless of how many questions a skeptic asks and has answered about God, sometimes they will never believe. If a person has determined that they don't want to be under the authority of the Creator, their skepticism will often mask this desire for autonomy. At some point in their life a person will have to honestly deal with the answer to the questions they've asked before they ask more. If someone wonders if God exists, and that question is answered satisfactorily, it would be important to stop for a moment and consider the ramifications of having that question answered in the affirmative.

Think of it like this: if I point to a laptop computer on my desk and you question whether the computer is real – let alone if it can do all that I claim it can - then I'm effectively being asked to prove it. If I then turn on the computer and proceed to demonstrate a software application, the first question has been answered. You may have additional questions that I may or may not be able to answer. It is entirely appropriate to wonder about how a computer works, and it is likely that I won't be able to explain microchip technology. However, this doesn't change the fact that the computer is real and it works. Just because there remain unanswered questions doesn't negate the reality of the laptop's existence.

In the same way, if it is reasonably argued that God exists, there may be additional questions that will be asked. But something significant has been accomplished that is often overlooked by quickly accessing the next database of skeptical questions. At some point a skeptic may discover that there may never be an end to the questions, because they have no intention of following God, even if the questions were all answered (which will never happen).

A key point of reflection would be when a person asks and answers the question about whether Jesus Christ was literally brought back to life after being crucified in 33 A.D. This watershed moment of faith requires a person to honestly evaluate whether they're predisposed to reject Jesus Christ. In my experience, when the faith chips are down, I end up back at this very simple apologetic for belief in Jesus and for believing God's Word. Simply put, by Jesus being brought back from the dead, he verifies His claim to deity and is found truthful because He prophesied that this would happen. *Romans 1:1-4* states:

Paul, a servant of Christ Jesus, called to be an apostle and set apart for the gospel of God— the gospel he promised beforehand through his prophets in the Holy Scriptures regarding his Son, who as to his human nature was a descendant of David, and who through the Spirit of holiness was declared with power to be the Son of God by his resurrection from the dead: Jesus Christ our Lord.

It is because Jesus Christ was resurrected from the dead, and ascended into heaven in front of eye witnesses (see *1 Corinthians 15:5-7*) that we have confidence that everything He said was "God's Word" because He was God in the flesh. It is because of the resurrection that we're sure that he is truly the Lord and know that when he suffered death on the cross he could actually qualify to be the innocent scapegoat for our sins. Anyone who wasn't perfect deity would deserve to die for their own sins and couldn't be substituted for someone else. It is because of the resurrection of Jesus Christ that we know that the testimony of His apostles is true and that the words they wrote down have the authority and power of Holy Scripture. Apart from the supernatural act that is the resurrection of our Lord Jesus, he wouldn't be a Savior who satisfied God's justice and we'd be guilty of worshipping a dead human being.

This is the essence of the Apostle Paul's teaching in *1 Corinthians 15:13-17:*

If there is no resurrection of the dead, then not even Christ has been raised. And if Christ has not been raised, our preaching is useless and so is your faith. More than that, we are then found to be false witnesses about God, for we have testified about God that he raised Christ from the dead. But he did not raise him if in fact the dead are not raised. For if the dead are not raised, then Christ has not been raised either. And if Christ has not been raised, your faith is futile; you are still in your sins.

Simply put, if you assume God exists then you can logically posit that He is all-powerful. If He is all-powerful then it is no big stretch for Him to do miracles, chief among them would be raising Jesus from the dead. Whether He did resurrect Christ and whether He could resurrect Christ are two separate questions. The first is a question of historical fact.

The second is a question about the existence of God. Christian believers should never feel silly for believing in God, for many non-Christians around the globe can tell by nature itself that there was a creator. It is foolish to believe that we exist because of a cosmic series of chance occurrences. There are a number of great resources to address the questions that skeptics have on this and other subjects. Two books I can recommend are *The Reason for God*, by Tim Keller, and *If God is in Charge*, by Steve Brown. Through these books, you'll discover that logic and belief are not always contradictory propositions.

I'd also like to encourage you to access two websites that are full of wonderful resources for Christian students: *thirdmill.org and www.desiringgod.org.* The first is an online ministry begun by Dr. Richard Pratt. The second is the website of Dr. John Piper of Bethlehem Baptist Church in Minneapolis, Minnesota. He has written a reasonable and easy-to-understand defense of why evangelicals rely upon and believe the Old and

New Testaments to be the authoritative Word of God. When you visit the site, check out the resource section titled, "Why We Believe the Bible."

On many occasions I have spoken with friends who weren't Christians and they would cite various supposed contradictions in Scripture (most of which were easily explained), or the hypocrisy of Christian leaders over the centuries (many of which are indefensible), and other objections to Christianity that had absolutely nothing to do with the person of Jesus Christ. Inevitably I would bring them back to a critical theological cross road and ask this question: "If in 33 A.D. Jesus Christ was genuinely, physically resurrected from the dead, is he then someone who needs to be acknowledged and do His words need to be taken seriously?"

I completely agree with my unbelieving friends, not to mention the Apostle Paul, that if Jesus Christ isn't truly physically alive that the entire Christian faith is a hoax. If Jesus isn't really God then we didn't have an ample substitute for our sins and we'll still be judged guilty for them and suffer their due punishment. However, if He is alive then He is in a class by himself.

As the writer of the book of Hebrews teaches, Jesus is superior to not just the Old Testament heroes but to the angels in heaven. *Hebrews 1:1-4* states:

> *In the past God spoke to our forefathers through the prophets at many times and in various ways, but in these last days he has spoken to us by his Son, whom he appointed heir of all things, and through whom he made the universe. The Son is the radiance of God's glory and the exact representation of his being, sustaining all things by his powerful word. After he had provided purification for sins, he sat down at the right hand of the Majesty in heaven. So he became as much superior to the angels as the name he has inherited is superior to theirs.*

All of this to say that if you don't have substance to your faith, if you haven't built your theological house upon the foundation of God's Word, you will not survive the storm that is coming your way on the college campus. From the classroom to the dorm room and many places in between, the details of my belief system were challenged on campus. It is a war that I believe is waged by our spiritual adversary, Satan.

Hear me correctly on this point: I don't believe that people who challenge our beliefs are evil or Satan's minions. *Ephesians 6:10-12* says:

> *Finally, be strong in the Lord and in his mighty power. Put on the full armor of God so that you can take your stand against the devil's schemes. For our struggle is not against flesh and blood, but against*

*the rulers, against the authorities, against the powers of this dark world
and against the spiritual forces of evil in the heavenly realms.*

Our enemy isn't the people challenging our beliefs but
the evil one who would like us to ignore that which is obvious to
us. God is real, He is powerful, and because of Jesus we now
have the physical evidence that we need to see with our own
eyes that He is gracious and compassionate, slow to anger, and
abounding in love.

You don't have to intellectually bury your head in the
sand and you certainly don't have anything of which to be
ashamed regarding your belief in God's existence. Very few
people are true atheists, defined as completely not believing in
the existence of God. *Romans 1:18* teaches that our desire to live
autonomously from God and His moral prescriptions makes us
suppress the truth.

Humble Christians understand this truth in their own
experience because they have to suppress thoughts about God's
presence in order to wander into behavioral territory that they
know is morally out of bounds. So, how did we get to this place
of caring about what God thinks and others haven't? Why have
we believed and others who have heard the same message
haven't? It's humbling and amazing. It's called grace.

Amazing Grace...How Sweet!

I've got a heavy right foot. Many times the police have reminded me of this since I turned 16 and got my driver's license. More times than I'd like to admit I've been pulled over for speeding and asked for my license and registration. The routine is always the same, too. I get pulled over, they ask for my information, then as quickly as the patrolman walks away to their cruiser to check my record, I begin praying that I'll get a break. There is a five-minute period where I hope that I'll be treated mercifully, not being given what I truly deserve: a speeding ticket. Most of the time, justice is served and I'm fined for my lawlessness. However, there have been times when, for reasons unbeknownst to me, the police have let me go with a stern warning to slow down.

Most of my life I would have characterized being let off from getting a ticket as grace. However, what I experience when I don't get the punishment I deserve is really mercy. By contrast and compliment, "grace" is getting what I do not deserve. In this particular example, the police officer would not only return to spare me the punishment that I deserved, he or she would give me the keys to their own personal car as a gift that I didn't deserve. Grace is "undeserved favor." Historically, I always thought that differentiating between grace and mercy was theological hair splitting. I no longer think so.

I've come to the conclusion that Scripture teaches that we're only capable of believing in Christ when the Holy Spirit enables us to comprehend the truth of God's Word. Jesus said in *John 6:63-65*:

> *"The Spirit gives life; the flesh counts for nothing. The words I have spoken to you are spirit and they are life. Yet there are some of you who do not believe.' For Jesus had known from the beginning which of them did not believe and who would betray him. He went on to say, 'This is why I told you that no one can come to me unless the Father has enabled him."*

Once enlightened, once we're given eyes to see and ears to hear, then we're capable of professing faith in the risen Christ. Jesus said in *John 15:5, "Apart from me you can do nothing."* That includes our own conversion to the faith.

This reality has simultaneously humbled and comforted me. I'm humbled that God would not only spare me the punishment for my sins, but He would go the extra mile to help me see the truth of the gospel. Additionally, the presence of the Holy Spirit in my life gives me His joy, peace, and resulting strength to enjoy a life I don't deserve to live. Being a Christian isn't just "fire insurance" to avoid eternal hell. It is more than mercifully being spared punishment. Knowing Jesus is experiencing the wonders of His presence and the amazing grace of being His beloved child. But it all begins with God's effort to pursue His children. It ends with our submission to His Lordship.

I'm also comforted by the reality of His promise that He will never leave or forsake me. The truly converted person can take great joy in the reality that their salvation is a gift from God. We are not only mercifully forgiven for our sins, we are credited with Christ's righteousness and that is the means of our accomplishing of God's law.

We are completely justified in the presence of God because Jesus has not only satisfied God's wrath as it pertains to our past, present and future sins, but we are holy right now in the sight of God because of the atoning sacrifice of Jesus Christ. In other words, this test must be passed with 100% correct, and Jesus' grades are now credited to us as if we took the test and got an A+. *Romans 3:20-25* says:

Therefore no one will be declared righteous in his sight by observing the law; rather, through the law we become conscious of sin. But now a righteousness from God, apart from law, has been made known, to which the Law and the Prophets testify. This righteousness from God comes through faith in Jesus Christ to all who believe. There is no difference, for all have sinned and fall short of the glory of God, and are justified freely by his grace through the redemption that came by Christ Jesus. God presented him as a sacrifice of atonement, through faith in his blood.

Knowing that you're secure because of the finished work of Christ will protect you from the myriad of campus cults that prey on the uniformed student. Realize that any so-called church that tells you that you earn your salvation or keep your salvation by some act of righteousness on your part instead of humble faith in what Jesus had already done, that salvation would rob Jesus of the 100% credit due Him for saving you. If there is any one moral act that we can or cannot do that will tip the scales of God's justice either for or against us, understand that it is our one action and not Jesus that has ultimately saved us.

Cults and so-called Christian denominations which teach a works-oriented salvation (Our Good Works = Our Salvation) are plentiful on the college campus. They will entice you with the promise of a family under the guise of caring for you or they'll offer an ecstatic experience that they claim will empower your faith as never before. Once you've reached the emotional pinnacle of their community or begun to truly become dependent on that community, that's when you discover the bad news that you can never truly be secure in your relationship with God.

There are rules (written and unwritten) to be followed and activities to participate in if you want to strive for the elusive goal of security and peace with God. Ultimately, according to these groups, you can only truly be secure when you're performing perfectly. And since all truly honest people know that they're never performing perfectly and never will, they reasonably conclude that they can never be truly secure by virtue of their own efforts.

In his book *Transforming Grace*, Jerry Bridges wrote:

He (God) accepts you strictly by His grace through the merit of Jesus Christ alone. Such an unqualified statement about the love of God sounds exceedingly dangerous, leaving me open to the charge of saying in effect that God doesn't care whether you sin or not. But consider the alternative: 'God loves you if you are obedient and doesn't love you if you are disobedient. Since God's love is conditioned on obedience and you are never perfectly obedient, God never loves you perfectly or accepts you completely.' Such a bald description of the all-too-common works/merit way of thinking about our relationship with God puts the issue into focus. We are accepted by God, not only in salvation but also in our present relationship with him, either on the merit of Jesus Christ or on the basis of our own performance.[4]

---

[4] Bridges, Jerry, *Transforming Grace* (Colorado Springs, CO: NavPress, 1991), pg 87-88.

Security in Christ and Loving God

Perhaps you think it's a matter of semantics to say that good works follow genuine faith instead of saying that good works produce a saving faith. I disagree. Why? Because why we do what we do is as important as what we do (don't feel badly if you had to read that sentence more than once).

Consider this scenario: I want to buy a large new plasma television for my home office but I have to get my wife's consent first to spend our money on such an extravagance. In order to butter her up, I vacuum the house, do the dishes and clean up the garage. When she comes home and sees all the hard work I've done, she is initially thrilled with the effort and appreciative. Then I spring the trap and ask her if she's okay with me buying this $2,000 television. At that point she realizes that all of the work she thought was done out of love for her was really done to manipulate her into giving me what I wanted.

Our motive for obedience to God is why I believe so strongly that not only do we not do good works to earn our relationship with God but also that we can't do anything to jeopardize our standing with Him once we're genuinely converted. If I'm obeying the Lord for any other reason than to simply bring pleasure to His heart (including out of fear that I might lose my relationship with him and eventually go to hell), then that act of "righteousness" is not an act of love but one of selfishness designed to get something from Him or keep Him from doing something I don't want.

The gift of God's grace in Christ enables us to do what we would naturally be unable to do on our own: love Him. Once liberated from the fear of eternal death, once freed from the condemnation that would come from sinful actions, the child of God can now appropriate His power through His Holy Spirit and obey His Word as an act of love for Him. *John 14:20-21* says:

> *"On that day you will realize that I am in my Father, and you are in me, and I am in you. Whoever has my commands and obeys them, he is the one who loves me. He who loves me will be loved by my Father, and I too will love him and show myself to him."*

Loving God is expressed through obedience. Obedience must be spurred by grace or else our works are a means of trying to manipulate God. The person who doesn't love God doesn't know Him, as articulated by the Apostle John in *1 John 4:7-10*:

> *Dear friends, let us love one another, for love comes from God. Everyone who loves has been born of God and knows God. Whoever does not love does not know God, because God is love. This is how God showed his love among us: He sent his one and only Son into the world that we might live through him. This is love: not that we loved God, but that he loved us and sent his Son as an atoning sacrifice for our sins.*

If someone claims to be a Christian but doesn't want to please God, they are not a genuine believer. Being a genuine believer doesn't mean that we won't sin or struggle, it just means that in our hearts our disposition has changed and we now want to bring pleasure to our Heavenly Father's heart.

You might be surprised to find out just how few churches believe the gospel as I've explained it in this chapter. That's why it is so important to search carefully for both a campus ministry and a local church that teach the truth of God's Word. "Spiritual Orthodoxy" is a phrase used to describe churches that are vibrant and alive with a passion and love for God, but are doing so within a framework of a rational, Biblical theology. Too often, college students from home churches with traditional worship styles will on campus get their first exposure to contemporary praise and worship services at churches that teach doctrine that is sometimes very close to if not clearly heretical.

On the other end of the spectrum, some Christian students are very quick to judge churches or campus ministries that have non-traditional forms of worship. At the end of the day, it is the Protestant Reformation's mantra of "Sola Scriptura" or "Scripture Alone" that must be our credo. Scripture must be the foundation of our view of the world. The Word of God must dictate and advise our choices of friends. The Bible must be the final authority about whom we date and with whom we share the most intimate parts of our lives. The Old and New Testaments must inform our understanding of ourselves, our understanding of God, and they must inform the way we worship and love our Savior. I've always loved this proverb of King Solomon:

Trust in the LORD with all your heart and lean not on your own understanding; in all your ways acknowledge him, and he will make your paths straight.
Proverbs 3:5-6

RANDOM TIP D
Watch out for the Debt Demons

Before going to college the credit card companies didn't pursue you because they don't want your parents anywhere near you when they sign you up. At an festival or athletic contest on campus, someone will be standing at a kiosk or under a tent, offering you a free t-shirt or other prize in exchange for signing up for their credit card. It sounds like a great deal.

Here's the catch: in exchange for no monthly charge, they will give you a credit line of a few thousand dollars that you can use to borrow from them by simply swiping your credit card wherever and whenever you want. See an outfit you like? Swipe it. See the latest electronic device or cell phone accessory? Swipe it. All the way up to your credit limit. Sounds like the freedom to buy what you want and pay for it later, right?

Wrong. It's not freedom. It is a prison. The credit card they are willing to give you has an interest rate that, at times, can be as high as 20%, which means that the monthly balance (the money you've borrowed but have yet to repay) is going to have tacked on to it an interest charge. In this case, 20% of the value of the balance divided by 12 months.

In other words, if you have an outstanding balance of $1,000, each month you let that go unpaid, the generous credit card company will add another $16.50 to it. If the $1,016.50 isn't paid off the next month, they add another $16.95 to the $1,016.50 for a grand total of $1,033.45. And on and on it goes until you're buried under debt. Even if the initial interest rate is low, it will skyrocket the first time your payment is late or once the introductory period ends.

It is in the best interest of these profit-motivated credit card companies to get you on the hook for thousands of dollars by the time you graduate. They make their money off of your interest payments. What do they care if in the process they ruin your credit score and make it difficult for you to buy your first car after college, and next to impossible for you to buy a home any time soon. Short term versus long term gain is often what college is about. Take King Solomon's words to heart from *Ecclesiastes 5:10*:

Whoever loves money never has money enough; whoever loves wealth is never satisfied with his income. This too is meaningless.

www.threetips.com

Conclusion
How Will You Prepare?

As far as I can tell, there are three possible responses for a reader of this book who considers themselves a Christian student: apathy; arrogance; or anxiety. Let me encourage you to consider what your response truly is. In so doing, you may further prepare yourself for your college experience.

Apathy

If you're not buying into the seriousness of what's lying ahead for you in terms of spiritual battle and can't really get into what I'm saying about what's coming your way on campus, it may be a good time to reevaluate how serious you are about following Jesus. Perhaps a parent, pastor or a peer gave you this book to read and you've already determined in your heart that you plan to live life outside of Christian community at college. You already feel bubbling inside of you a curiosity that will drive you to experiment with the world's temptations. I'll tell you what I've told students over the years: according to the Scriptures, your disobedience to God's Word will result in one of two things – neither is good and one is downright awful.

Hebrews 12:4-11 says:

In your struggle against sin, you have not yet resisted to the point of shedding your blood. And you have forgotten that word of encouragement that addresses you as sons:

"My son, do not make light of the Lord's discipline, and do not lose heart when he rebukes you, because the Lord disciplines those he loves, and he punishes everyone he accepts as a son."

Endure hardship as discipline; God is treating you as sons. For what son is not disciplined by his father? If you are not disciplined (and everyone undergoes discipline), then you are illegitimate children and not true sons. Moreover, we have all had human fathers who disciplined us and we respected them for it. How much more should we submit to the Father of our spirits and live! Our fathers disciplined us for a little while as they thought best; but God disciplines us for our good, that we may share in his holiness. No discipline seems pleasant at the time, but painful. Later on, however, it produces a harvest of righteousness and peace for those who have been trained by it.

If you are a child of God in rebellion to God, you can expect discipline that will be painful. I know the sting of my Heavenly Father's loving hand, and I'll tell you that it's not something you want to experience if you don't have to...and you don't. You can obey Him. You choose not to do so. *1 Corinthians 10:13* states that God is faithful and won't allow us to be tempted beyond what we can handle. He will provide a way out for us, if we desire to love and obey Him.

On the other hand, you may discover that you don't love God or want to follow His direction and commands. What is worse than discipline for a person that considers themselves a Christian? No discipline at all. Why? Because that person may discover that they weren't truly a Christian to begin with. "Getting away with it" may feel exhilarating at the time, but it may be evidence that you were never truly indwelled by God's presence. God's lack of discipline in your life could reveal that you weren't a child of His to begin with. Getting chastened by God so we can share in the joy of living as He intended is a painful process, but nothing compared to the pain of an eternity in hell. That's what waits for the person who is an illegitimate child whom the Lord doesn't discipline.

I understand this. When my kids were little I would take them to the public playground so they could run around. There was always some undisciplined little brat running around hurting other kids and making a scene. Their weak parent usually was sitting to the side watching their little hellion make everyone else miserable. As many times as that scene unfolded in front of me (and it did often), I never once felt the compulsion to intervene and discipline a child who wasn't my own. Although I must confess that there was a time or two I wanted to put the child's parent over my knee and give their fanny a good whack!

According to *Hebrews 12*, God is not in the business of disciplining children who aren't His own. You get to find out one of two things in your rebellion and neither of them are good things to discover.

Arrogance

My chief concern for certain Christian students – particularly the ones who are private Christian schooled or home schooled all the way up to college – is that they would come to campus not really believing that they could fall into the kinds of temptations I've described in this book. If this is the case for you, I'm more frightened for you than for anyone else, because as King Solomon taught, *"Pride goes before destruction."* (*Proverbs16:18*)

Time and time again I've seen genuine believers who grew up in great homes, under great parental and pastoral training, display remarkable overconfidence and nonchalance in their approach to temptation. I also have seen quite a bit of arrogance demonstrated by students who think they are "better" Christians comparatively because they don't find what others struggle with particularly tempting to them.

Allow me to warn you that this lack of humility is not only a precursor to your own spiritual tumble into difficulty, but that your sin of pride and self-righteousness is just as offensive to God as drunkenness or sexual immorality. In fact, I see Jesus demonstrating a remarkable level of patience for prostitutes and drunkards by comparison to the religious zealots who thought themselves better than the really bad "sinners." The former he had compassion for because they were so lost; the latter he called a bunch of snakes (see *Matthew 3:7, 12:34 and 23:33*).

Anxiety

Perhaps after reading the stories and testimonies of students who failed miserably at the spiritual battle on campus, your reaction is one of great fear for what lies ahead. You now are scared that it is possible for you to go to college and fall away from the Lord. To that let me echo the advice of Strider (later revealed to be Aragorn) on his first encounter with Frodo Baggins in *The Fellowship of the Ring*:

Strider: Are you frightened?

Frodo: Yes.

Strider: Not nearly frightened enough.

You should be concerned about the dangers ahead, just like you should be concerned about casually strolling across a freeway of speeding cars. To not be concerned for your safety would be utter foolishness. The spiritual battle on campus is 100% real and the casualties of the war are too many to count.

One of my best friends has a personalized license plate that reads simply, "BE ALERT." He didn't just get this plate to encourage others on the road to drive carefully. More generally, he got it to remind himself and the rest of us of what the Scriptures tell us about being alert about the spiritual battle.

1 Peter 5:5-11 says:

All of you, clothe yourselves with humility toward one another, because, "God opposes the proud but gives grace to the humble." Humble yourselves, therefore, under God's mighty hand, that he may lift you up in due time. Cast all your anxiety on him because he cares for you.

Be self-controlled and alert. Your enemy the devil prowls around like a roaring lion looking for someone to devour. Resist him, standing firm in the faith, because you know that your brothers throughout the world are undergoing the same kind of sufferings.

And the God of all grace, who called you to his eternal glory in Christ, after you have suffered a little while, will himself restore you and make you strong, firm and steadfast. To him be the power for ever and ever. Amen.

God doesn't want you to walk around filled with anxiety about how life is going to turn out, but He does want you to be alert to the dangers inherent to your spiritual life that are all around you. In that case, as we humble ourselves, he will empower us to withstand the onslaught of temptations and attacks of our enemy the devil.

Fight Like King Jehoshaphat

My favorite Old Testament narrative is the story of Jehohaphat, King of Israel. In so many ways and on so many different levels this story encapsulates the life of the Christian and our struggle to depend completely on God for our spiritual safety. Again, this is a lengthy passage of Scripture, but I promise you'll be glad your read it. Enjoy this account from *2 Chronicles 20:1-25*

After this, the Moabites and Ammonites with some of the Meunites came to make war on Jehoshaphat.
Some men came and told Jehoshaphat, "A vast army is coming against you from Edom, from the other side of the Sea. It is already in Hazazon Tamar" (that is, En Gedi). Alarmed, Jehoshaphat resolved to inquire of the LORD, and he proclaimed a fast for all Judah. The people of Judah came together to seek help from the LORD; indeed, they came from every town in Judah to seek him.
Then Jehoshaphat stood up in the assembly of Judah and Jerusalem at the temple of the LORD in the front of the new courtyard and said:

"O LORD, God of our fathers, are you not the God who is in heaven?
You rule over all the kingdoms of the nations. Power and might are in
your hand, and no one can withstand you. O our God, did you not
drive out the inhabitants of this land before your people Israel and give
it forever to the descendants of Abraham your friend? They have lived
in it and have built in it a sanctuary for your Name, saying, 'If
calamity comes upon us, whether the sword of judgment, or plague or
famine, we will stand in your presence before this temple that bears
your Name and will cry out to you in our distress, and you will hear us
and save us.'

"But now here are men from Ammon, Moab and Mount Seir, whose
territory you would not allow Israel to invade when they came from
Egypt; so they turned away from them and did not destroy them. See
how they are repaying us by coming to drive us out of the possession
you gave us as an inheritance. O our God, will you not judge them?
For we have no power to face this vast army that is attacking us. We do
not know what to do, but our eyes are upon you."

All the men of Judah, with their wives and children and little ones,
stood there before the LORD.
Then the Spirit of the LORD came upon Jahaziel son of Zechariah, the
son of Benaiah, the son of Jeiel, the son of Mattaniah, a Levite and
descendant of Asaph, as he stood in the assembly. He said:

"Listen, King Jehoshaphat and all who live in Judah and Jerusalem!
This is what the LORD says to you: 'Do not be afraid or discouraged
because of this vast army. For the battle is not yours, but God's.
Tomorrow march down against them. They will be climbing up by the
Pass of Ziz, and you will find them at the end of the gorge in the Desert
of Jeruel. You will not have to fight this battle. Take up your positions;
stand firm and see the deliverance the LORD will give you, O Judah
and Jerusalem. Do not be afraid; do not be discouraged. Go out to face
them tomorrow, and the LORD will be with you.' "

Jehoshaphat bowed with his face to the ground, and all the people of Judah and Jerusalem fell down in worship before the LORD. Then some Levites from the Kohathites and Korahites stood up and praised the LORD, the God of Israel, with very loud voice.

Early in the morning they left for the Desert of Tekoa. As they set out, Jehoshaphat stood and said, "Listen to me, Judah and people of Jerusalem! Have faith in the LORD your God and you will be upheld; have faith in his prophets and you will be successful." After consulting the people, Jehoshaphat appointed men to sing to the LORD and to praise him for the splendor of his holiness as they went out at the head of the army, saying: "Give thanks to the LORD, for his love endures forever."

As they began to sing and praise, the LORD set ambushes against the men of Ammon and Moab and Mount Seir who were invading Judah, and they were defeated. The men of Ammon and Moab rose up against the men from Mount Seir to destroy and annihilate them. After they finished slaughtering the men from Seir, they helped to destroy one another.

When the men of Judah came to the place that overlooks the desert and looked toward the vast army, they saw only dead bodies lying on the ground; no one had escaped. So Jehoshaphat and his men went to carry off their plunder, and they found among them a great amount of equipment and clothing and also articles of value—more than they could take away. There was so much plunder that it took three days to collect it.

Jehoshaphat was a warrior, a king, the son of a king and a man of great wealth and power. He was not a wimp nor was he a spiritual weakling. The Chronicler tells us that he faithfully followed the Lord and gave great concern for the commands of the Lord. This was a man's man.

Yet we see three distinct characteristics in Jehoshaphat's life that we would be wise to emulate. First, in the face of an enemy too large for him to fight he recognizes that he cannot face this alone. He calls together the people of God for prayer and fasting, so they together can depend on one another during this time of crisis.

2 Chronicles 20:3 states, "*Alarmed, Jehoshaphat resolved to inquire of the LORD, and he proclaimed a fast for all Judah.*" There is nothing wrong with being scared or anxious, for even the tough kings of Israel knew when they were facing something that they had no ability to do alone.

Jehoshaphat's second trait is that he's aware of his weakness and inability. It would be easy for a warrior who had many previous victories to assume that he would be able to fight the upcoming battle in the same way and win. Jehoshaphat did not make the mistake of overestimating his own strength.

In tremendous act of public humility, verse 12 of *2 Chronicles 20* records that the King stood in front of his people and prays, "*O our God, will you not judge them? For we have no power to face this vast army that is attacking us. We do not know what to do, but our eyes are upon you.*" The king admitting that he didn't have power and that he didn't know what to do? That kind of humility is counterintuitive to proud people. But it was a realistic assessment for Jehoshaphat. Humble people are just honest about whom they are and what their capabilities are, and the Scripture says that those are the people whom God, by His power, will assist. It is the proud that God opposes (*1 Peter 5:5*).

What is most amazing about Jehoshaphat and the third characteristic of his life is His willingness to trust the Lord's solutions to His problems instead of proudly coming up with his own. *"This is what the LORD says to you: 'Do not be afraid or discouraged because of this vast army. For the battle is not yours, but God's."* The prophet's words in *2 Chronicles 20:15-16* hold great significance for us as Christians. Not simply because God promises that He will win the battle through His methodology, but that the battle is His to fight in the first place.

Imagine how difficult it would have been for the King to have God give him this instruction instead of "Here's a battle strategy, Jehoshaphat, go here and do this and that, and here are the weapons you'll need, and you're going to take these guys down." God tells the Israelites to simply take up their positions and they will see the hand of the Lord. And they do.

The underlying beauty of this passage is that it is a wonderful picture of the Gospel of Jesus Christ. A foe we are unable to fight threatens to destroy us, and God tells us that He will fight the battle for us. He sends His Son who destroys death and eliminates the enemy for us through His righteous act, and we're only required to take up our place of faith and trust that His work will be sufficient for the victory over our enemy.

The only way we win the war over sin and death is to humbly come to God and completely trust that His battle plan is the only one that will work. Once we surrender our pride and admit that we cannot save ourselves, all that is required of us is to submit by faith to His gracious offer of salvation. In the end, the battle is the Lords and He goes before us to deliver us from evil. He does the work, he gets the credit and glory, and we can rest easy and celebrate because we know that our Savior, Jesus Christ, is the victor.

Johnny Came Marching Home

Jon was raised by a Christian family, received Christ at an early age, came through my youth ministry in Tallahassee and then went off to a prestigious private university. Like so many Christian college students, he faced the temptations of excessive drinking. He lived on a dorm hall and in an apartment with young men who didn't know Jesus. These relationships would prove challenging to his own behavior.

His ROTC class had very few Christian men, so he often found it easy to behave as his fellow "soon to be soldier" friends. He also had a high school sweetheart whom he dated throughout his college years. Those are particularly challenging dating relationships, too, because the longer you're together, the deeper your passion is for each other and the more abundant the opportunities to struggle with sexual temptation.

After graduation Jon went to Iraq to serve in the Army, working to liberate the Iraqi people through Operation Iraqi Freedom. Fully trained by the Army to survive in a hostile environment, Jon found himself in some dangerous situations. On one occasion, friends of his were killed when a road side bomb exploded. Jon was on the scene to see the nearly disintegrated bodies of his fellow serviceman.

One other time, Jon was the gunner on a transport vehicle while the convoy he was part of made its way through the heart of Baghdad. As they traveled down the highway and approached an underpass, Jon noticed that a civilian vehicle was speeding down the onramp and would possibly be on a collision course with their lead vehicle. As he was trained to do, Jon fired his machine gun across the front windshield of the perceived threat. Once the driver of the vehicle noticed the tracer fire come across his window, and that he was about to unknowingly merge into the path of an armed U.S. military convoy, he very quickly slammed on his breaks. Can you imagine what a frightening experience that would be for a civilian? His mother probably made him wash his own pants that day.

In spite of numerous encounters in a hostile combat environment, early in 2007 Jon finished his tour of duty and returned to our hometown without physical injury. His family and friends were overjoyed. Jon arrived in Florida with vast experience in organizational leadership, married to his high school sweetheart, the father of a baby boy, and took a position as the new CFO of a local business. He later was hired by the FBI and now serves our country as a Federal Officer. After nearly a decade away from college, Jon came marching home and God had grown him up to be a fantastic man of the Lord.

It wasn't until Jon had been home a couple of months that it dawned on me that Jon had made it through two wars safely: one for his life and country in Iraq, and one for his soul at his university. So how did he do it?

It started in high school before he ever ventured out to be a college student. Jon diligently pursued an increasing understanding of what he believed. When he realized that he'd be going to college at the same school as a close friend from our church group, he made certain that they would be roommates.

They both had high school girlfriends, they would both live amongst the crazy party atmosphere of their university, but they would do it together. Together they held each other accountable. Together they prayed for forgiveness when they blew it.

Jon and his roommate also made a concerted effort to attend church and their campus fellowship. He made it a priority to develop an entirely new set of Christian friends whom he could encourage and who in return could spur him on toward love and good deeds. Jon's long-term girlfriend was a wonderful, beautiful Christian woman. Through all of their struggles to please the Lord by obeying His commands regarding sexuality, they never lost sight of Christ and His desire for their lives. It was a great day when they married, and his college roommate stood with him to celebrate the moment.

Jon's roommate and he also had a clear understanding of who they were: broken sinners with the natural inclination to please themselves rather than God or others. Given their humility, they were certain not walk into too many situations where they'd be overwhelmed by temptation. These brothers also knew what they believed, so they were able to resist the intellectual assault on their deeply held religious convictions.

There is one more detail that I think is worth mentioning: Jon's roommate and best friend was Andrew, the man mentioned in our Introduction. In many ways this survival guide is merely a tracking of how these two brothers made it spiritually through their college years and came out the other side prospering as believing adult men, loving husbands, doting fathers, and diligent servants of God.

My college years were incredible for me. I grew spiritually in ways that I never thought possible, and I did so at one of America's notorious party schools. That intense environment of partying and craziness sharpened my spiritual instincts, helping me to see and understand that temptation wasn't something with which I wanted to flirt. Through my friends at my campus ministry, through the fellowship of my church, by way of a growing comprehension of my sinfulness and God's graciousness, and a desire to please God that resulted from His kindness, I survived and thrived at the state university.

With Christ you can do so much more than simply survive the challenges ahead of you, but with serious preparation and adherence to these Three Tips for spiritual survival, you can make it through college and in the end be a stronger and more mature Christian because of all of your experiences.

And isn't that what's important about our exciting life adventures? We want to enjoy them, but we also want and need to survive in order to tell our stories to other people.

Prism CHURCH

an ACTS29 Network Mission

SHINING *the* **LIGHT** *of* **GOD'S GRACE** *and* **LOVE**
TO LOS ANGELES AND THE WORLD

---

prismchurch.com

Pastor Chuck & Carolyn Ryor

ACTS29
N E T W O R K

JOIN US AND BE PART OF THE MISSION!
PRISM CHURCH • PO BOX 70677 • PASADENA, CA 91117

Appendix – How to Become a Christian

Let me state plainly what should have been clear from the beginning: this book is written for Christian students. If you don't have a genuine relationship with God there is little value to these tips. You will not gain any points with God in eternity because you followed any of these guidelines.

Nonetheless, somewhere in the course of reading this book you may have asked the question, "Am I really a Christian?" Perhaps you know that you are not, but no one has ever adequately explained to you how you would go about becoming one. So let me briefly attempt to summarize what it means to be a Christian and how to become one.

Becoming a Christian is not like purchasing insurance to protect you from some future malady: come to Jesus and avoid hell. In that case we would be using God to get something we want from Him. Instead, it is a relationship, built on understanding, trust, and interaction with our heavenly Father.

God created us to have a relationship of perfect harmony with Himself and His creation. We opted for doing our own thing in our own way; this is the essence of what the Bible calls sin. This selfish inclination and need to be autonomous from God has separated all human beings from

God because He is holy and we are not. This "fall," or banishment from His presence, makes sense because if purity is mixed with impurity, it is no longer pure. 100% pure spring water would cease to be 100% pure if a single drop of polluted water was added to it. In the same way, a perfectly pure, holy God couldn't remain in the presence of an impure person.

This predicament may seem a harsh judgment from an impatient and angry God. However, God is completely just for demanding that we perfectly obey His laws and perfectly just for judging us guilty for both our nature to sin and for the actual acts that result from having that nature. "Fair" would be God properly judging guilty those who are guilty and punishing them accordingly. If this appears bleak, it's understandable. But there's good news: God is both just and merciful.

God desired a renewed relationship with us and had compassion on those in His creation. In His divine plan, God purposed to save us from our separation from Him by sending a substitute to pacify His need for justice and to purify a people from their sins so they would be clean in His holy presence. The catch is that the only perfect person is God Himself, so the only solution would be to send His only begotten son. His son, Jesus Christ, was part of His being from all eternity, not created as we were, and thus He had a perfect nature and was completely holy.

Hence, when Jesus of Nazareth died on the Roman cross in 33 A.D., He was not simply suffering a martyr's death for what He taught and believed; He was being punished for the sins of everyone who would ever look to Him for forgiveness for their sins. When a person looks to Jesus and receives the gift of His presence in their lives, they are both forgiven for their sins (past, present and future) and they are credited with Jesus' perfect obedience to the law so they will now be completely holy in God's presence for all of eternity.

Eternal life starts the day you receive, by God's ability and through your faith, the Holy Spirit of God and begin a relationship with the Father. We are not worthy to enter into a relationship with God on our own merits, because we would fail in any attempt to live out perfectly the laws of God. God the Father knew this, so He and His Son executed a rescue plan whereby Jesus would perfectly obey the law, deserve the eternal presence of the Father and the Spirit by His good works, and give up this right for our salvation.

God loves His children and wanted relationship with them. However, His holiness demanded that these children be 100% pure before entering His presence. Now, through our trust in Christ's sacrifice for us, His blood cleanses us from sin (meaning that Christ's blood satisfied the wrath of God). Jesus' blood represents the final payment of a just God for the lives of His children who needed to be bought back from a certain eternal death outside of His presence. Jesus paid the price for our sins. Jesus was an "atoning" sacrifice, a scapegoat who took the brunt of God's Holy wrath so those who trust in Him would never have to and could rest easy in the presence of their Heavenly Father.

Now that the offer of forgiveness and cleansing has been made, all that is left to do is to reach out and receive this gift by faith. It is a simple act of prayer, calling on the Lord to apply to you the payment for sins that was made in Christ. And as a result, you begin a relationship with God that will last for all eternity. It is a gift of His grace and mercy that you cannot earn. You can only humbly admit your need for Christ and rely on Him only.

A person who truly enters into a relationship with God will have in her a desire to love and please God, not so she can achieve a relationship with Him or so she can stay in a relationship with Him, but because she has been loved and saved by Him. A Christian has been saved by His grace and goodness, so secure and loved by God and promised a relationship for all eternity that they are compelled in gratitude to live a life of good works for Him. Read and enjoy this passage from *Ephesians 2:1-10*:

As for you, you were dead in your transgressions and sins, in which you used to live when you followed the ways of this world and of the ruler of the kingdom of the air, the spirit who is now at work in those who are disobedient. All of us also lived among them at one time, gratifying the cravings of our sinful nature and following its desires and thoughts. Like the rest, we were by nature objects of wrath. But because of his great love for us, God, who is rich in mercy, made us alive with Christ even when we were dead in transgressions—it is by grace you have been saved. And God raised us up with Christ and seated us with him in the heavenly realms in Christ Jesus, in order that in the coming ages he might show the incomparable riches of his grace, expressed in his kindness to us in Christ Jesus. For it is by grace you have been saved, through faith—and this not from yourselves, it is the gift of God—not by works, so that no one can boast. For we are God's workmanship, created in Christ Jesus to do good works, which God prepared in advance for us to do.

Today, you can begin a relationship with God and know that He will never abandon you, in spite of mistakes you make and sins you commit. You will be saddened when you displease your gracious Father and, from time to time, He will discipline you as any good parent would, but He is committed to relationship with you and to forming your life to reflect more of the character of His Son Jesus, your Savior.

"Faith" is expressed through personal prayer. I encourage you to come to God in conversation. He has promised to hear your prayers, and this prayer in particular is one that brings joy to the Father, Son, and Holy Spirit. In fact, the Scriptures teach that when a person turns to God from his own way—something the Bible calls repentance—and he receives Christ as his Savior and Lord, a joyous celebration takes place in heaven.

Do you want to begin a relationship with God? To do so would bring joy to Him and all who are in His presence in heaven. If so, pray a prayer similar to the one that follows, and if you genuinely do so, you will be spiritually reborn. *Romans 10:9-11* states:

If you confess with your mouth, "Jesus is Lord," and believe in your heart that God raised him from the dead, you will be saved. For it is with your heart that you believe and are justified, and it is with your mouth that you confess and are saved. As the Scripture says, "Anyone who trusts in him will never be put to shame."

The starting point for the relationship with your Heavenly Father begins right here, and you'll never need to start it again.

PRAYER TO BEGIN A RELATIONSHIP WITH GOD

"Dear Heavenly Father, I have a nature that is rebellious and in my heart I want to be worthy of a relationship with you through my own good works, so I can be proud of myself.
But I cannot live your law perfectly, so I deserve to be punished.
However, God, thank you for not abandoning me to be punished for my sins. Thank you for desiring a relationship with me and making the perfect provision to forgive me for my sins through the work of your Son, Jesus. Today, by faith, and through your undeserved kindness, I receive Jesus as my Savior.
Thank you for your sacrifice. Thank you for loving me.
Help me to please you and know you. Amen."

If you prayed that prayer, the Scriptures say that you are now a child of God. Celebrate and shout for joy because your sins have been forgiven, never to be remembered, and you have entered into the relationship for which you were originally created. This is a relationship of love with your Heavenly Father through the perfect work of His Son, Jesus Christ, and sealed forever by the presence of His Holy Spirit who now lives in you and will be with you. Read this assurance from *Ephesians 1:13-14:*

And you also were included in Christ when you heard the word of truth, the gospel of your salvation. Having believed, you were marked in him with a seal, the promised Holy Spirit, who is a deposit guaranteeing our inheritance until the redemption of those who are God's possession - to the praise of his glory.

At the risk of being repetitive, I have three tips for you growing closer to your Heavenly Father now that you've begun a relationship with Him; discover, depend, and deepen.

1) Discover the joy of having Christian friends walk the path of faith along side of you. You need other Christians to grow spiritually.

2) Depend on the power of the Holy Spirit, who now lives inside of you. You do not naturally have the strength to live the Christian life. You need the power of His fullness in your life. Ask Him to fill you each day.

3) Deepen your understanding of God's Word. You will need to study the Scriptures to grow in your understanding of God's grace and love.

If you apply these three tips, Scripture says that God will use them as a means of His grace to bless you and draw you closer to Himself and more into Christ likeness. And when you make mistakes and do things you know you shouldn't, immediately confess your sins to God and celebrate that someone has already been punished for those sins. Jesus Christ.

My prayer for you is a mere echo of the Apostle Paul's prayer for the Christians in *Ephesians 3:14-19*:

For this reason I kneel before the Father, from whom his whole family in heaven and on earth derives its name.
I pray that out of his glorious riches he may strengthen you with power through his Spirit in your inner being, so that Christ may dwell in your hearts through faith.

And I pray that you, being rooted and established in love, may have power, together with all the saints, to grasp how wide and long and high and deep is the love of Christ, and to know this love that surpasses knowledge — that you may be filled to the measure of all the fullness of God.

www.threetips.com

About the Author

Chuck Ryor is the Lead and Teaching Pastor at Prism Church of Los Angeles, located in Pasadena, California. Prism is a non-denominational church that is part of the Acts 29 Network of Churches. Chuck has served for nearly two decades in student ministry and church planting, most of that in one of America's quintessential college towns, Tallahassee, Florida.

In addition to his ministry in Southern California, Chuck travels widely speaking to adults and students. Through his "THREE TIPS" seminars and "threetips.com" website, Chuck shares his campus experiences and insight with students in order to help them navigate the exciting, challenging and spiritually dangerous terrain of the college campus.

Educated at Florida State University, Reformed Theological Seminary and West Virginia University, Chuck worked as a disc-jockey and radio sportscaster before going into full-time ministry. He has also served as an Adjunct Professor of Communication at Providence Christian College in Ontario, California.

Pastor Chuck and his wife, Carolyn, have two children and live near Pasadena, California.

Stay connected with Chuck and the other members of the THREE TIPS Team through

THREETIPS.COM!

Register online for <u>FREE</u>.

Connect with others, get Three Tips gear and gather important campus survival resources.

- Chuck's Weekly College Blog
- Student Stories from around the country
- "Chick Tips" from female campus leaders
- LIVE Q & A online
- Random Tips and interviews from campus leaders throughout the U.S. and the world

SIGN UP TODAY AND STAY CONNECTED TO YOUR ONLINE SOURCE FOR CAMPUS SURVIVAL TIPS!

three tips

FOR CAMPUS SURVIVAL

Contacting Chuck Ryor

To schedule Chuck Ryor to speak at your church, school, conference, or to conduct his one-day seminar on the book's subject matter, contact Prism Ministries at 877-677-7476 (877-67-PRISM).

To order more copies of Three Tips for Campus Survival, visit www.threetips.com or contact Prism Ministries at 877-677-7476.

To follow Chuck online you can visit these sites:

www.threetips.com	Official Website
www.chuckryor.com	Chuck's Blog
www.prismchurch.com	Online Home of Prism Church of Los Angeles

You can also follow Chuck on Facebook and Twitter.

RED MOUNTAIN BOOKS®
www.redmbooks.com